End-of-Life Care and Pragmatic Decision Making

A Bioethical Perspective

D. MICAH HESTER

University of Arkansas for Medical Sciences

CAMBRIDGE UNIVERSITY PRESS
Cambridge, New York, Melbourne, Madrid, Cape Town, Singapore,
São Paulo, Delhi, Dubai, Tokyo

Cambridge University Press
32 Avenue of the Americas, New York, NY 10013-2473, USA

www.cambridge.org
Information on this title: www.cambridge.org/9780521130738

First published 2010

Printed in the United States of America

A catalog record for this publication is available from the British Library.

Library of Congress Cataloging in Publication data

Hester, D. Micah.
End-of-life care and pragmatic decision making : a bioethical
perspective / D. Micah Hester.
    p. ; cm.
Includes bibliographical references and index.
ISBN 978-0521-11380-9 (hardback) – ISBN 978-0-521-13073-8 (pbk.)
1. Terminal care – Moral and ethical aspects.   2. Terminal care – Decision
making.   I. Title.
[DNLM: 1. Terminal Care – ethics.   2. Bioethical Issues.   3. Decision
Making – ethics.   4. Palliative Care – ethics. WB 310 H588e 2010]
R726.8.H475   2010
179.7 – dc22   2009020441

ISBN   978-0-521-11380-9 Hardback
ISBN   978-0-521-13073-8 Paperback

End-of-Life Care and Pragmatic Decision Making

A Bioethical Perspective

End-of-Life Care and Pragmatic Decision Making provides a philosophical framework based on a radically empirical attitude toward life and death. D. Micah Hester takes seriously the complexities of experiences, and argues that when making end-of-life decisions, healthcare providers should pay close attention to the narratives of patients and the communities they inhabit so that their dying processes embody their life stories.

Every one of us will die, and the processes we go through will be our own – unique to our own experiences and life stories. Hester argues that it is reasonable to reflect on what kinds of dying processes may be better or worse for us as we move toward our end. Such consideration, however, can raise troubling ethical concerns for patients, families, and healthcare providers. Even after forty years of concerted focus on biomedical ethics, these moral concerns persist in the care of lethally impaired, terminally ill, and injured patients.

Hester discusses three types of end-of-life patient populations – adults with decision-making capacity, adults without capacity, and children (with a specific focus on infants) – to show the implications of pragmatic empiricism and the scope of decision making at the end of life for different types of patients.

D. Micah Hester is Associate Director of the Division of Medical Humanities and Associate Professor of Medical Humanities and Pediatrics at the University of Arkansas for Medical Sciences, and is clinical ethicist at Arkansas Children's Hospital. He is the author and editor of eight books and numerous journal articles, and he coordinates the Pediatric Ethics Consortium and the Pediatric Ethics Affinity Group of the American Society for Bioethics and Humanities.

To Caroline: I was never able to touch you when you were alive, but you touched me too deeply to express in words. Our special gain also became our greatest loss, and yet your story lives on with us always.

Contents

Preface

Any experience[, ideal, or concept], however trivial in its first appearance, is capable of assuming an indefinite richness of significance by extending its range of perceived connections. Normal communication with others is the readiest way of effecting this development, for it links up the net results of the experience of the group and even race with the immediate experience of an individual.

John Dewey

On the way
we passed a long row
of elms. She looked at them
awhile out of
the ambulance window and said,

What are all those
fuzzy-looking things out there?
Trees? Well, I'm tired
of them and rolled her head away
William Carlos Williams

Another book about end-of-life issues . . . how can this be? For more than thirty years, bioethics, medical ethics, clinical ethics (whatever you choose to call this field of concern) has been looking at end-of-life issues as paradigmatic of ethically challenging situations in medicine. For that long, at least, articles and books looking into the many aspects and challenges of end-of-life care have been produced. I cannot truly explain why I have added another text into this array.

And yet it is worth taking just a moment to note that there is always more to say about end-of-life care. We will all die. In fact, everyone who at the time of this writing is my age or older will be dead by the turn of the century. Today, tomorrow, and the next day, some physician will be at the bedside of some patient who is dying, and tomorrow (or maybe the next day) some patient's dying process will pose a challenge to herself or others – whether the challenge is medical, social, personal, psychological, or ethical. And surely somewhere in the United States during the next month, the end-of-life care considerations of a patient will prove ethically challenging to such an extent that it will be brought before a hospital ethics consultant or committee. These are inescapable facts of the world we live in. There truly is more to say, more work to be done. Given these facts, the book you hold does not pretend to have a final say or to produce the last word or even to be comprehensive.

During the preparation of the final manuscript for this book, two books, CG Prado's *Choosing to Die* and Robert Young's *Medically Assisted Death*, were published by Cambridge University Press. These two philosophers (Prado from Canada and Young from Australia) have offered careful and interesting arguments for "rational suicide" and "voluntary active euthanasia," and I recommend them to any reader of this book. While they are more narrowly focused in scope than this book, they both are more detailed in the development of their respective issues. What follows in these pages, then, may best be seen as a survey of how a radically empirical philosophical approach affects our analysis of (and practices surrounding) some specific issues in end-of-life care writ large.

What is equally important to distinguish, however, is the role philosophy plays in this book. In a review of Prado's and Young's books in the *Journal of the American Medical Association*, Ernle Young observed, "Prado's book is a . . . somewhat arcane academic treatise; Young's is a book of relevance to clinicians. . . . Prado's appeal to medical ethics will be appreciated only by the small minority of trained philosophers among them. . . . Young's book, in contrast, is a pragmatic and cogent read for all those [interested in bioethics]" (Young 2008,

1703). Now, whether or not I endorse the reviewer's take on these books, my point in mentioning this contrast between Prado and Young is to explain that the work you are now reading is somewhere in between. The early chapters are explicitly and purposefully philosophical – attempting to explain the conceptual basis that grounds the insights throughout the book. The later chapters turn to more clinically grounded discussions, though not devoid of philosophical text. I admit that I am unapologetic about this, as I believe good medical ethics demands a clear conceptual approach. And I trust that philosophers and clinicians alike will find herein challenging but useful considerations worth taking the time to read. (Of course, those less interested in the theoretical can skim Chapters 2 and 3.)

In sum, my work here takes on related lines of argument that follow from a particular philosophical attitude – that of radical empiricism. That is, this book is written by someone who wants to explore the implications for end-of-life care should we take on a concern for meeting the many and various textures of lived experience in their individual and social manifestations. If you are not so moved by the implications of a radically empirical attitude, I fear you will give up on the arguments herein within one or two chapters. I would not say that you were wrong to do so; only that it would be so much the worse for me if you did.

However, should you choose to take the journey, my hope is that you will find an account of morally sensitive care for the dying that, while possibly surprising – even infuriating – does, at least at times, help illuminate some truths about our living and dying. Life contains moments of hope and situations of deep tragedy, and what I believe is important for all of us to recognize is that life continues all the way to death – that is, that dying persons still live until their last moments. As such, we need to take seriously what such experiences entail for them, for the communities in which they reside, and for the persons and institutions that care for and about them.

I will let the rest of the book speak for itself, and for me.

As already noted, the subject matter has been covered extensively in the literature, and thus, many excellent pieces of analysis and insight simply have not been considered in this study. I regret that the book is impoverished all the more because of this. While the book is fashioned as a single, connected statement, it began in bits and pieces, fits and starts. One chapter of my original doctoral dissertation was the genesis of this work, and other journal articles and conference presentations took on related themes that came together in a more intentional and systematic way herein. All has been rethought in light of the general purpose of the book and the continuing flux of information and analysis concerning end-of-life medicine and practice.

I owe my deepest appreciation to a great many people, and though I may leave some important folks out, I want to let you and them know of their direct and indirect contributions to the completion of this work.

First, I must thank Michael Hodges, my dissertation advisor at Vanderbilt. The chapter on end-of-life care was his favorite of the dissertation, and as such, his encouragement in getting me to continue my work on the themes therein was of singular importance. Also, the influence of other graduate teachers, John Lachs and Richard Zaner, are evident throughout the text. I can only hope I have served their tutelage well.

As with much of my work, once again, John J. McDermott played a pivotal role in bringing this text to press. John heard a conference paper of mine, and at a subsequent luncheon suggested to me that coupling that paper with some of my previous publications would make a good book – I hope that I succeeded in creating just such a book. His support and friendship are always a great service to me.

Many people have read portions of this text, whether in early incarnations as journal articles or book chapters, or later as my attempt to complete the book came to a close. I would therefore like to thank the following publishers and publications for kindly granting me permission to draw on previously published writings of mine: Delease Wear, former editor of *Journal of Medical Humanities*, which published my first writing on end-of-life issues, now part of Chapters 3 and 4, and which originally appeared under the title "Progressive Dying: Meaningful Acts of Euthanasia and Assisted Suicides" in *Journal of Medical Humanities*, 1998, Vol. 19, no. 4:279–98; Glenn McGee, editor of the book *Pragmatic Bioethics*, which included two chapters of mine, one of which is the basis for parts of Chapters 4 and 5, and originally published in *Pragmatic Bioethics*, 2nd edition, Glenn McGee (editor), MIT Press, copyright © 2003, 121–36; Lainie Ross, editor of a special issue of *Theoretical Medicine and Bioethics*, from which an article of mine has become part of Chapter 6, and which originally appeared under the title "There is More to the Story than We Explicitly Acknowledge" in *Theoretical Medicine and Bioethics*, 2007, Vol. 28:357–72; Eve DeVaro Fowler former philosophy acquisitions editor at Rowman & Littlefield, which published my first monograph in bioethics, *Community as Healing*, in which some of the arguments of Chapter 2 were first developed and published: *Community as Healing*, copyright © 2001, Rowman & Littlefield 47–66; Worth Hawes, philosophy acquisitions editor at Wadsworth, which published my co-authored book *On James*, in which much of the "radical empiricism" discussion was first developed and published: *On James*, Talisse, RB, and Hester, DM, copyright © 2004, Wadsworth, a part of Cengage Learning, Inc., reproduced by permission, www.cengage.com/permissions; and anonymous reviewers of the many journal publishers to which I submitted material. Robert Talisse helped me fashion some of the work on James's radical empiricism (and attempts to keep me honest and reflective as a philosopher), and Chris Hackler read through several of the later chapters. Others who have influenced the work have been colleagues (in no particular order – with many I have forgotten to list, I'm sure) from around the country – Mary Mahowald, Griff Trotter, Toby Schonfeld, Karen Kovach, Alissa Swota, Tomi Kushner, James Medd, Mark Moller, David Mathis, Robert LaGrone, Harold Katner, Richard Ackermann, and the anonymous reviewers of the various versions as this book tried to find its feet. To all of them, my deepest thanks. I owe special thanks to Beatrice Rehl at Cambridge University Press for her encouragement and championing of the book, and to Ronald Cohen, whose editing polished and improved the text.

I also wish to thank both my previous institution, Mercer University School of Medicine, and my current ones, University of Arkansas for Medical Sciences and Arkansas Children's Hospital, especially Bonnie Taylor, for their support of my professional scholarship. It is also at these two institutions where the majority of my clinical experience has arisen, and working with the physicians, nurses, and social workers, not to mention, patients and families therein, has enriched my understanding of these issues.

Finally, my family allows me the opportunity to work in the field that I do, taking time away from them to complete such efforts. My love and affection to Kelly, my wife, and to Emily, Joshua, Matthew, and dear Caroline, my children.

> ...And in the end
> The love you take
> Is equal to the love you make.
>   Lennon and McCartney,
>   *Abbey Road* (1969)

1

Crito Revisited

Socrates:... [K]eep this one truth in mind, that a good man cannot be harmed either in life or death, and that his affairs are not neglected by the gods....

Plato's Apology

Crito:... Socrates, I do not think that what you are doing is just, to give up your life when you can save it, and to hasten your fate...

Socrates:... We must... examine whether we should act in this way or not, as not only now but at all times I am the kind of man who listens only to the argument that on reflection seems best to me. I cannot, now that this fate has come upon me, discard the arguments I used; they seem to me much the same. I value and respect the same principles as before...

Plato's Crito

In the ancient Greek dialogue, *Crito*, Plato provides a portrait of his mentor, Socrates, only days before his death, and while the death scene itself is left to another dialogue, it is in *Crito* that Socrates explains why he would rather die in prison than live in exile (Plato 1997). The conversation is instructive on many levels, and one aspect that merits greater attention is the extent to which Socrates's cultivated character relates to the decision at hand. In particular, the dialogue raises issues concerning decisions at the end of life, decisions faced (in admittedly much different ways) by a multitude of patients, patient families, friends, and healthcare providers. In order to bring this out, let us begin, rather than with a simple recounting of the Platonic dialog, with a retelling of the story, updated and transformed from the prison cell to the hospital room.

Mr. S. is in his early seventies. He is a professor of philosophy and a war veteran who has earned commendations for bravery in battle, but is now confined to a bed in a hospital. According to his physicians, his cancer – a myeloma – is terminal, and so he simply awaits his fate. Though staring squarely into the abyss of death, his mind remains clear, even vibrant, and his mood is easily buoyed by visitations from his friends and loved ones.

One morning, Mr. S. awakens to see his friend and oncologist Dr. C., who has come not only to visit but to bring news and a proposition. The news is that Dr. C. has been investigating options, and clearly the hospital has reached the limits of what it can do to keep Mr. S. alive. In light of this, Dr. C. has looked into the possibility of employing alternative therapies at other centers around the world, and he wants to propose to Mr. S. some of these treatments that, while expensive and experimental, offer a small chance of success for extending life. However, being such a longtime and close friend, Dr. C. knows that Mr. S. will not be easily persuaded by some fly-by-night, desperate attempt to spare his life. Instead, Mr. S. will require of Dr. C. a careful accounting of this plan and a justification for following through with its recommended actions. In fact, Dr. C. is prepared to put forth several arguments on behalf of his proposition in the hope that Mr. S. might wish to prolong his life if possible.

According to his own evaluation of the situation, Mr. S. has been careful to cultivate the particular life he has led. He accepts the choices he has made, and most were quite deliberate. He has never been one to cling to life at all costs, and he does not jump at options simply because they are before him. He prefers to be reflective and to consider options in the context of his environment and character. As death approaches, then, he is confronted with the possibility, though perhaps remote, that he can stave off the abyss for awhile. Rhetorically, Dr. C. asks his friend, "Are you not acting 'cowardly' by taking the 'easy way out,' not fighting to extend your life ('Where is your rage against the dying of the light?')? Would it not mean more time with family and friends, and Don't you owe your family at least that much? Would you not be able to bring your unique insights to even more people as you continue to live? Would it not demonstrate a 'manly' defiance at the cruel fate that has befallen you?"

For Mr. S., none of the arguments is persuasive; in fact, Mr. S's responses are quite clear and consistent: His family will understand, and his friends surely should. There is no way of telling whether his unique way of interacting with others will translate outside the community in which it was formed. Why be defiant against a fate that was neither of his own choosing nor of his own making? To "scramble" for life is inconsistent with his approach to life. He has never wanted to be too self-concerned, never feared death, never wanted more than his due, never wanted to be beholden to others. He has always tried to think through problems and choose wisely, not wildly. Though death will surely be an outcome of his choices on these matters, it is a death he is willing to embrace, for it is the most meaningful way for him to live unto death.

How We Die

Life – *living*, really – is the condition in which we all find ourselves, and though there might be a few who vainly argue the opposite, and regardless of the promises of a few geneticists or even some cryogenicists, *that* we *die* is a fate that most of us realize. However, these two facts taken together often lead to stress and frustration concerning our futures. Death is inevitable, whereas living is actual. Living is what we know; death is obscure. Eventually, though, it is possible to come to grips with one important fact: Even though death is the end point of our living embodiment, dying is a process within embodied living itself – that is, dying is part of our on-going life stories. Should this realization occur, the focus may shift from *that* we die to *how* we die.

Illustrating what she calls the "cinematic" myth of the "Good American Death," Nancy Dubler writes, "[The death scene often] includes the patient: lucid, composed, hungering for blissful release – and the family gathers in grief to mourn the passing of a beloved life. The murmurs of sad good-byes, the cadence of quiet tears shroud the scene in dignity" (Dubler/Nimmons 1992, 146). Unfortunately for many of us, our deaths will not be the spiritual, peaceful "passing" that we might envision or desire. As physician Sherwin Nuland explains, "To most people, death remains a hidden secret. . . . [T]he belief in the probability of death with dignity is our, and society's, attempt to deal with the reality of what is all too frequently a series of destructive events that involve by their very nature the disintegration of the dying person's humanity" (Nuland 1993, xv, xvii). For many, the hope is that they will die surrounded by loved ones (or quietly in the night), slipping away without pain after tying up all loose ends. The reality for the great majority of us, however, is that we will find ourselves ravaged by disease, struck down by illness, or tragically injured; we will be hooked up to machines, ingesting drugs. Nurses and physicians, strangers to us really, will be our most consistent contacts with humanity. Family and friends will find themselves without resort and at a loss to help if for no other reason than that we rarely give a clear account of our desires concerning end-of-life care before it is too late to give any account at all. We would like to think that these situations are at the margins, but if so, the margins are awfully wide and, either way, must not be ignored. Death, as William Gavin has argued, is a complex of historical and cultural as well as biological factors that do not present themselves for tidy packaging (see Gavin 1995; 2003). Crudeness and vagueness, frustration and mutilation are at play as much as scientific, technological precision in diagnosis and prognosis. Loneliness, pain, and bitterness are more common than peace and joy.

Mr. S, then, is a rare person – thoughtful, brave, and consistent in his character, able to move toward death with a calm, careful, considered disposition. In these respects, his case is easily idealized, hardly displaying the confusion, pathos, and tragedy of the hundreds of thousands of patients each year who find themselves confronting issues at the end of life. As such, there is only little we can glean from Mr. S's situation. Tolstoy's Ivan Ilych may be closer in sketch to many real-world deaths, with his pains and fears, concerns and insights, and yet his account also marks the death of only one man. What can we learn from any one death? Alone, maybe not much, but situated within a continuum of cases, we may be able to garner some insights.

To illustrate a particular continuum of dying patients, allow me to recount a few stories previously published by others.

Approximately forty years ago, then medical student Sherwin Nuland on his first night in the hospital encountered a dying patient, James McCarty. Recalling the situation, Nuland writes:

James McCarty was a powerfully built construction executive whose business success had seduced him into patterns of living that we now know are suicidal. But the events of his illness took place [at a time] . . . when smoking, red meat, and great slabs of bacon, butter, and belly were thought to be the risk-free rewards of achievement. He had let himself become flabby, and sedentary as well. . . .

McCarty arrived in the hospital's emergency room at about 8:00 p.m. on a hot and humid evening in early September, complaining of a constricting pressure behind his breastbone that seemed to radiate up into his throat and down his left arm. . . . The intern who saw McCarty in the emergency room noted that he looked ashen and sweaty and had an irregular pulse. . . . The electrocardiographic tracing . . . revealed that an infarction had occurred, meaning that a small area of the wall of the heart had been damaged . . . .

McCarty reached the medical floor at 11:00 p.m., and I arrived with him. . . . As I walked onto the division, the intern, Dave Bascom, took my arm as though he was relieved to see me. " . . . I need you to do the admission workup on this new coronary that's just going into 507 – okay?" . . . .

McCarty greeted me with a thin, forced smile. . . . As I sat down at his bedside, he suddenly threw his head back and bellowed out a wordless roar that seemed to rise up out of his throat from somewhere deep within his stricken heart. He hit his balled fist with startling force against the front of his chest in a single synchronous thump, just as his face and neck, in the flash of an instant, turned swollen and purple. His eyes seemed to have pushed themselves forward in one bulging thrust, as though they were trying to leap out of his head. He took one immensely long, gurgling breath, and died. (Nuland 1993, 3–5)

In another story, James Buchanan discusses the circumstances surrounding Alzheimer's victim, Murray Wasserman.

The third stage of Alzheimer's is surely the most benevolent, the most understanding and merciful, of death's trimesters. All the confusion, embarrassment, and agony of self-observation are forfeited in favor of grateful amnesia.

Family and friends become strangers while the familiar and foreign lose the elasticity of their boundaries and become one....

For survival, only simple tools are needed: air, food, water. Life at its most basic and most elementary level has no need for anything unnecessary and burdensome. Murray simplified all that he had become for the purpose of concentrating what little he had on that which remained. Indeed, he was a child again. His bowels and bladder were liberated from social customs.... Rules and regulations ... were abandoned in favor of more immediate concerns. He had become a child again.

Of course, his friends and family saw none of this. Rather, they saw an old, emaciated man who wore diapers and wept to himself alone, and sometimes cried in grateful acceptance of the slightest things....

Murray was engaged in a desperate struggle for his life, for his existence, for some shred of solidity against the possibilities of death and nothingness.... [E]very minute, every hour, every day was a desperate struggle to remain something against forces that sought to make him nothing....

In the end, all death comes from anoxia.... One tries not to breathe, to end it all quickly, but the body is too desperate to obey such intellectual suicide. It wants to live even if the brain desires to die. And so like a heaving straining animal, the frightened lungs continue again and again their futile effort until coma and unconsciousness discontinue this malice of self-observation and self-torture.

Murray died in such a way; he died wrapped about himself – actually holding on to himself for dear life – in a fetal position. Were it not for the gray hair, the wasted six-foot body, the wrinkled and puffy face, one might have thought him a child who died of crib death.... But Murray Wasserman was not a child but rather an old – very old – man who died before his time and looked far more ancient than his sixty years could ever foretell. (Buchanan 1989, 45–50)

Finally, author and physician Richard Selzer tells of his encounter with an AIDS patient and his partner in 1990.

At precisely 4 P.M., as arranged, I knock on the door. It is opened by ... let him be Lionel, a handsome man in his late thirties.... He is an ordained minister.... In the living room Ramon is sitting in an invalid's cushion on the sofa, a short delicate man, also in his thirties. Ramon is a doctor specializing in public health – women's problems, birth control, family planning, AIDS. He is surprisingly unwasted, although pale as a blank sheet of paper.... He and Lionel have been lovers for six years....

For a few minutes we step warily around the reason I have come there. All at once, we are engaged. I ask him about his symptoms. He tells me of his profound fatigue, the mental depression, the intractable diarrhea, his ulcerated hemorrhoids. He has Kaposi's sarcoma. Only yesterday a new lesion appeared in the left naso-orbital region. He points to it. Through his beard I see another, larger black tumor. His mouth is dry, encrusted from the dehydration. He clutches his abdomen, grimaces. There is the odor of stool.

"I want to die," he announces calmly without the least emotion. (Selzer 1992, 284)

The common thread among these three stories is simply that death is rarely clean, hardly ideal; as Gavin points out, "death – or more *non*-precisely speaking, dying – remains at least somewhat wild-game flavored" (Gavin 2003, 107). Also, the character of each person's death is shaped by her history and community. Furthermore, these cases illustrate a continuum present among specific acts of dying, a continuum that ranges from deaths where control is not a factor to those where controlled manipulation is not only possible but preferable.

James McCarty killed himself through his own extravagant living, an unintended "suicide" as Nuland put it. He died in one powerful instant, alone with an inexperienced medical student left to fend for himself. In a very important sense, we can also say that there is no way his death could have been otherwise. Though he may have had control over his eating and living habits before his heart gave out, once McCarty found himself in the hospital, it was simply too late. Control over his death was clearly not at issue.

Murray Wasserman, on the other hand, reveals the very real distance between one's situation and the perceptions of others. An old man dies like a child, while his relatives find him pathetic and decrepit. Fighting for a self he long ago lost, however, Murray dies as alone as McCarty, lost in a world of his own. And here one could argue that so much more could have been done. The progressive nature of Murray's disease allowed for the possibility of proactive measures aimed at determining the dying process on a personal level. Advance directives and communication among health care professionals, family, friends, and of course Murray himself during the early stages of the disease might have helped with care in the later stages.

Finally, Ramon's situation illustrates a desire to avoid the emptiness of the previously described deaths. Influenced by the nature of his profession and the character of his relationships, Ramon was keenly aware of the issues involved in his own disease. Committed to a loving relationship, his desire to die also was concerned with his partner, the burdens involved in care, and the embarrassment of continued existence in this state. Ramon seized the opportunity to exercise his agency, wishing to participate in his own dying process.

With this continuum – ranging from an utter lack of, to an expressed desire for, control over dying – squarely in our minds, let us return briefly to Mr. S. More clearly than most, Mr. S's situation demonstrates a fundamental position taken in the pages of this book: The dying process is part of lived experience. Of course, every death demonstrates this in its own way, but for some, taking charge of the process in a *meaningful* way is possible.[1] Furthermore, the choices and actions that are sought (if not enacted) in pursuit of meaningful dying are morally charged, and significant. Finally, the ability to engage one's own dying process, to make it not simply anathema to living but constitutive of one's character, in short, to embrace it as part of one' s life story, may result in a morally appropriate choice to die even in the face of alternative ways to continue living.

Engaging the Dying Process: Meaningful Life Stories

Engaged dying brings meaning to what may seem to be otherwise meaningless acts and choices. Such meaning-making is grounded

---

[1] The case of Mr. S. is surely a glorified account, but a meaningful death need not be one of peace and ease (though our myth of the "good death" may suggest as much). The death of Susan Sontag, as recounted by her son David Rieff, is one of pain and agony while battling cancer. And yet her death did have meaning for her, as she determined to fight for every last minute of life she could. As Rieff recounts, her doctor said, "'If you want to fight, if what matters to you is not quality of life . . .' And my mother said, 'I'm not interested in quality of life.'" (interview in Salon.com; http://www.salon.com/books/feature/2008/02/13/david_rieff/index1.html). In his book, Rieff discusses Sontag's earlier successful bout with stage-4 breast cancer: "For as the years went by, my mother began more and more to think of her survival . . . as the result of medical progress and also of her willingness to have the most radical, mutilating treatment. . . . *As she understood her own story*, choosing the milder version . . . would have meant not making the commitment to survival that was required. Real commitment for her was always radical" (Rieff 2008, 38; emphasis mine). And later, he notes about her final struggle with cancer, "[S]urvival was her goal , and that never changed from the moment of her diagnosis to almost the hour of her death" (82).

in the recognition that living continues unto death. That is, lived experience continues for those who are dying, and like all other moments in life, the lived experience of dying can, at times, be shaped by our own hands.

The approach to living and dying assumed in this book is itself grounded on what philosopher William James calls "radical empiricism." While the next chapter is dedicated to elucidating this concept, in brief we can say here that "radical empiricism" accepts as "real" any and all experience, and thus requires that all experience be taken seriously. Furthermore, "experience" is characterized as a flowing, fluctuating stream. Both this continuity of experience and need for serious attention to relationships that arise in experience require a view of our lives that, while noting those moments of discontinuity and the possibility of novel, radical change, also attends to connectedness of our memories, histories, choices, and actions. Value, itself, arises in experience, not imposed upon experience from some transcendent realm of value. Our lives range from birth to death, and everything in between is what we call *living*. Radical empiricism is a philosophy that focuses simply on *that*. As such, it is well suited (if not uniquely so) to approach issues in the care of dying patients. It is not unimportant, but often forgotten, that the dying process is part of living. This fact is often de-emphasized or misplaced when we are confronted with a dying patient, because our attention so quickly turns to the end of the process – namely, death – without significant attention to the intervening living that goes on until the end is reached. However, as Gavin points out, "[J]ust as one would not identify a melody with the last note in the score, so too one should not focus on the last moment of dying, that is death, at the expense of the entire process of dying." (1995, 123) This is no trivial observation. Such a view demands an attitude toward dying that treats it as continuous with the rest of our living. In fact, the end itself is part of the context set forth by what comes previous to it. In another use of a musical example, Erich and Roberta Loewy (2000) note that

If the preceding movements [of Beethoven's ninth symphony] had been less majestic, if they had failed to prepare the ground properly, our perception of the last movement would have been quite different.... In dealing with issues at the end of life, then, we cannot take that life out of the context of its history, of its social setting or its existential being. (5–6)

Mixing metaphors, though death and dying do mark the "final" chapter of our life stories, it is still part of the book – a situated and significant part, at that – and it gains meaning from the chapters that precede it.

The goal of health care itself is often colloquially defined as avoiding death, preserving life, but surely this focus is far too narrow. Such a take on the aims of medical practice is not only doomed to failure, since we shall all die someday, but is far too negative to prove practically helpful in the daily lives of physicians and patients. Thus the end of medicine must first and foremost be positive and progressive, attaching to the reality of active engagement in the world. Elsewhere, I have proposed that "living healthily" should be medicine's primary goal for the patients it serves, since this goal not only captures the historical calling of physicians, but also the needs and desires of patients (Hester 2001). Furthermore, living healthily taken as a positive, contextually sensitive goal can be achieved with patients at any point along life's spectrum. In fact, it is not only possible but morally significant that dying patients can live healthy lives unto death. If this sounds oxymoronic, then we must develop a stronger understanding of what is meant by "living healthily."

While I refer the reader to the more robust explanation of this position in the work *Community As Healing* (Hester 2001), briefly here, living healthily constitutes a person's active engagement in the world, in the decisions that affect her life, in the communities of which she is a part and are part of her. Such an engagement is participatory, when a person's interests and values find expression and are infused into the environment. Living healthily does not demand that a particular individual's interests and values always hold sway, but that they be taken seriously by the community because that individual participates as a member of the community. None of us is an atomic creature, insularly independent. We are, in fact, social products, our very selves arising from the communal interactions in which we take part. For medicine to take this seriously requires an expansive and flexible view of the goals of medicine in order to develop means appropriate to the ends to be achieved. It is a turn away from the negative concept of "cure" and passive concept of "consent" as fundamental and toward the positive, active ideas of "healthy living" and "participation." Such a turn values "meaningful" living, as such living stems from the patient's own life story and accepts the fact that patients can die meaningfully.

That is, the positions taken throughout this book, grounded by the arguments in Chapters 2 and 3, rely on a philosophy that takes the radically empirical attitude toward dying, and thus treats the dying process as a possibility for "meaning." "Meaning," I will argue, is not universal but particular. In the words of William James, meaning arises as the marriage of our "intelligently conceived ideals" with the fortitude necessary to achieve them. The intelligent development and pursuit of ideals is the act of living significantly, and significant living develops within the context of our narrative existences – put simply, our life stories. At first glance, this may look as if "meaning," conceived in this way is either voluntaristic or subjective, but it is not. Our life stories are open narratives, authored by ourselves *and* others, situated within communities and available to observation, review, and critique. These stories are not merely "subjective," because they arise from the language and customs of the community, and they feed and adjust into those same communal life stories. In this way, they are "objective" to the extent of their availability for critique and employment by others – that is, to an extent similar to anything else we might call "objective."

Not all dying can be meaningful, on these terms, and some processes will employ greater and lesser degrees of patient fortitude or ideal-generation. And yet such a view of dying with meaning can be positively illuminating for a great many situations that otherwise remain unnecessarily meaningless and underdeveloped.

Morally Appropriate Choices to Die: Meaningful Deaths

The moral implications of this position reach beyond patients themselves. They necessarily implicate physicians, nurses, other health-care workers, as well as family friends and institutions. The following chapters attempt to make a consistent and coherent argument concerning ethical decisions in end-of-life situations. In particular, Chapters 2 and 3, while setting forth considerations for (grounding) moral deliberation, will demonstrate that in some (I believe, few) cases, we can say that there are patients who will find/determine that they have an ethical obligation to die in meaningful ways, and that those who care about and for them are also obligated to aid in their dying processes.

Chapters 4 through 6, look at particular kinds of patients, from adults with full decision-making capacity to adults who, for a variety of reasons, are without capacity, to children and infants. These chapters illuminate the implications of the philosophical argument afforded in the next two chapters for many different kinds of dying patients. Of course, this cannot be an exhaustive attempt. The work you have before you is *not* intended to be both a taxonomy and a philosophy of end-of-life care; however, it illustrates a number of situations that patients find themselves in where ethical reflection can aid in decision making, and ground at least some decisions to hasten death even when medicine is capable of protracting the process.

2

Blindness, Narrative, and Meaning

Moral Living

[P]atients order their experience of illness – what it means to them and to significant others – as personal narratives. . . . To fully appreciate the sick person's and the family's experience, the clinician must first piece together the illness narrative as it emerges from the patient's and the family's complaints and explanatory models . . .

Arthur Kleinman

[N]one of us get [*sic.*] to write the final chapters of our lives as if we had nothing whatsoever to do with other people. Put more positively, most of us want to write that final chapter in a way that preserves the "best" values that have guided our lives up to that point.

Howard Brody

Chapter 1 sets forth the idea that dying is constitutively part of living, and living part of dying. Furthermore, it noted that not only is there a vast continuum of dying processes, but that in some cases, a dying process can be meaningfully controlled. The purpose, of this chapter is to spell out more thoroughly the philosophical and ethical positions that ground the arguments concerning care for the dying in the rest of the book. I begin with an elaboration on the details and meaning of "radical empiricism." I then take up William James's prophetic warning that each of us is blind to others' interests and values. However, the radically empirical attitude demands that we overcome the blindness. To do so, I employ insights from George Herbert Mead and John Dewey to fashion a narrative ethics that makes life stories the focus of moral deliberation and participation. The next chapter will then begin to employ these insights in order to help understand the moral context of dying patients.

Taking on the Radically Empirical Attitude[1]

In order to understand the philosophical underpinnings of this book – "radical empiricism" – it may help to place it in a larger philosophical context. We begin, with some questions: Is our world and our human nature compatible with goodness or evil? How do we know whether what we are doing (have done or will do) is good? What do we even mean when we say that something is good? Must some higher power (a god, if you like) *ordain* what is good, or would some higher power simply *recognize* something as good. Philosophers have long discussed questions just like these, trying to understand the "true" nature of the world and, as it affects moral thought, the "true" nature of values. Both metaphysically and morally, a deep concern for what is "ultimate" continues to arise – whether that be a concern for what is the ultimate nature of things or the ultimate values that ground morality. In general, the response to this concern can be divided, roughly, into two camps – monism and pluralism.

Monists are those who claim that at bottom the world is "one." What might this mean? Well, in today's post-Human Genome Project world, such a claim could be made about some geneticists. That is, some claim that all living things can ultimately be understood in and through their DNA. Whether we are concerned with hair and eye color, breast cancer, alcohol dependency, or sexual orientation, the basic understanding of the human condition will be available to us once we unlock all the complex mysteries of our genetic codes. Further, we might claim that the power of DNA is predicated on a basic view of the world as made up of bare matter that transacts according to the laws of science. Here, then, we would have a monistic belief

[1] The following section is adapted from Talisse/Hester 2004.

about the world – that ultimately we are nothing but bare matter – in the form of what philosophers call "scientific materialism."

Of course, monisms are not all "material" in nature. Sometimes they are expressed in terms of ultimate "substance" – mind or matter, god or perceptions; sometimes as ultimate "narrative" – historical progression or divine completion. Importantly, for our study, *ethical* monism can manifest itself as identified principles – categorical imperative or greatest happiness – or as ultimate sources – divine revelation or human nature.

Generally, then, we might say that monism "is the belief that somewhere, in the past or in the future, in divine revelation or in the mind of an individual thinker, in the pronouncements of history or science, or in the simple heart of an uncorrupted good man, there is a final solution" (Berlin 1969, 167).

In contrast, *pluralism* argues that neither the world nor our values are reducible to any one (set of) substances or principles or anything else. That is, no one vision, principle, or process can capture the vast and differing textures of the universe and the moral life. The world is not simply following scientific principles or divine commands. Our moral actions are not reducible to basic ethical tenets or simple conceptions of what is good.

Radical empiricism is a response to the competing philosophical positions broadly laid out by the concepts "monism" and "pluralism." Explicitly, William James states:

[A] short name to the *attitude* in question ... [is] radical empiricism.... '[E]mpiricism,' because it is contented to regard its most assured conclusions concerning matters of fact as hypotheses liable to modification in the course of future experience; and ... 'radical,' because it treats the doctrine of monism itself as an hypothesis, and, unlike so much of the half-way empiricism that is current under the name of positivism and agnosticism or scientific naturalism, it does not dogmatically affirm monism as something with which all experience has got to square. ([1897], 134 [emphasis added])

It is not unimportant to note that James speaks here of radical empiricism as an "attitude." That is, radical empiricism is an approach to philosophy and life, not a doctrine per se. Again, rather than emphasizing what we must believe the world *is*, radical empiricism begins as a *comportment* toward the world we inhabit. And what form does such comportment take? We are told that as empiricists, we must first take our conclusions about life to be "hypothetical" – that what we know today does not guarantee what will come tomorrow. But we must go further than this. We are enjoined not only to be empiricists, but to be "radical" as well. Thus we should avoid monism, not treating experience as ultimately reducible to one kind of thing, substance, or essence. No singular claim can capture the fundamental character of life. Experience is not one *thing*, but admits of plurality of things, concepts, and ideals.

Why take such an attitude? For James, radical empiricism avoids the problem of "intellectualism," which he describes as "the belief that our mind comes upon a world complete in itself and has the duty of ascertaining the world's contents; but has no power of re-determining its character, for that is already given" ([1911], 735). And why is intellectualism so dangerous? Simply put, it does not do justice to lived experience. That is, such a position loses touch with the very character of experience as it comes upon us. In fact, James says, no "given" or singular "nature" of experience exists prior to our engagements with the world, and our efforts continually add to, subtract from, shape, and re-shape the very "nature" of the universe. "It may be true that work is still doing in the world-process, and that in that work we are called to bear our share. The character of the world's results may in part depend upon our acts" ([1911], 736). Such a claim has significant consequences, for if the world is still in process and that process includes our actions and their consequences, each of us has significant responsibility for how the world actually comes out. At the same time, as empiricists, we cannot say with complete confidence ahead of time how our actions will affect the world around us – that is, we must recognize the possibility that we may, even with our best efforts, make matters worse.

Radical empiricism, then, is an attitude of neither determinism nor fatalism; further, it is neither pessimistic nor optimistic. It is, instead, a "melioristic" alternative to traditional philosophical accounts. That is, as James says, "a pluralistic universe's success ... [requires] the good-will and active faith, theoretical as well as

practical, of all concerned, to make it 'come true'" ([1911], 737).
It is thus important to note that radical empiricism is ultimately
a deep *human* psychological and philosophical *commitment* to two
claims (both of which will have bearing on ethics): (1) One must not
deny anything that is experienced, and (2) one must not deny the
potency of human action.

What exactly is meant by the notion that radical empiricism com-
mits one not to deny experience? In the history of philosophy, some
empiricists have insisted that our experiences are analyzable into
simple parts, broken down into almost atomic perceptions. You do
not, then, see and hold a red ball, but you perceive, individually, the
color red, the round shape, the springy rubber. But then how do you
get the experience we call "the red ball"? Such an atomistic account
of empiricism, while good at identifying aspect of experience, treats
each aspect as independent from each other – what David Hume
called "simple impressions." However, we are left with a puzzle – how
do simple impressions unite? Imagine, if you will, that you have pain
in your left arm. As experienced, can you separate the pain from
where it exists? That is, can you practically conceive of pain without
relating to the body that has it? If all we get are these basic perceptions, how can we ever have the experience of a complex thing –
this red ball or my arm pain? *Radical* empiricism, then, can be characterized as taking seriously that things *as experienced* are real. For
example, the experience of *my arm* pain is one complete experience
where the relationship expressed by the terms "my" and "arm" are
necessary to the experience of this "*pain.*"

As James insists, "To be radical, an empiricism must neither admit
into its constructions any element that is not directly experienced,
nor exclude from them any element that is directly experienced. For
such a philosophy, *the relations that connect experiences must themselves be
experienced relations, and any kind of relation experienced must be accounted
as 'real' as anything else in the system.*" ([1904], 195). A radically empirical attitude demands that we recognize as "real" not just immediate
sensations but *any experienced relation* as well; it attempts to be "true"
to experience by accepting experience as it comes – for example,
"this red ball," not simply "red," "round," "springy" each in turn.
As James says, "Radical empiricism . . . is fair to both the unity and

the disconnection. It finds no reason for treating either as illusory" ([1904], 197).

One last definitive discussion of "radical empiricism" solidifies the account:

Radical empiricism consists first of a postulate, next a statement of fact, and finally of a general conclusion.

The postulate is that the only things that shall be debatable among philosophers shall be things definable in terms drawn from experience. [Things of an unexperienceable nature may exist ad libitum, but they form no part of the material for philosophical debate.]

The statement of fact is that the relations between things, conjunctive as well as disjunctive, are just as much matters of direct particular experience, neither more so nor less so, than the things themselves.

The generalized conclusion is that therefore the parts of experience hold together from next to next by relations that are themselves parts of experience. The directly apprehended universe needs, in short, no extraneous trans-empirical connective support, but possesses in its own right a concatenated or continuous structure. (James [1909], 136)

James *postulates* that *only and all* experience matters to philosophy – radical empiricism establishes an attitude, an approach to philosophy writ large. Once such a vision of philosophy is postulated, a "fact" about experience itself is put forth – namely, the "parts" of experience include both "disjunctive" *and* "conjunctive" elements, and this "fact" leads to the "conclusion" that while experience is divisible, it is also constitutively self-supporting *in and through* its content. Ours, accordingly, is a "pluralistic universe," but rather than experience merely consisting of atomic sensations and isolated moments/events, James claims that this plurality includes the connections among sensations and events as well.

Thus, James metaphorically describes experience as a "stream" where sensations, thoughts, and the relations among them all flow together and yet are divisible for particular purposes – purposes developed and implemented by us in order to shape experience (James 1890, ch. IX). The radically empirical attitude accepts this account of experience as its starting point and, as we shall see later in this chapter and beyond, goes a step farther by placing the fate of the world and the very meaning of our lives in our own hands.

To summarize, radical empiricism is "empiricism" because:

1. It is pluralistic, starting in experience and building from parts to wholes.
2. It is fallibilistic, laden with risk, since we do not know what tomorrow will bring, and our pronouncements about the future are always tentative.
3. It is consequentialist because only when the future does play itself out will we know the "truth."
4. It is melioristic because how the future plays itself out is determined, in part, by our efforts.

It is "radical" because:

1. It recognizes that the connectives among the "parts" of experience are themselves experienced and experienceable.
2. It posits a continuum between means and ends founded on the constitutive relationship between the two.
3. It follows that consequences are not isolatable from the choices and actions that bring them to fruition.
4. It therefore believes that risk is assessable, maybe even assailable at times.

The radically empirical attitude has direct consequences for the moral life. The remainder of this chapter, as well as the next, will spell these out in some detail, but a brief synopsis follows:

1. To follow radical empiricism, all experience matters, experience is wherein value arises, and the whole of moral experience is not available to any one person. Moral experience manifests a plurality of values, irreducible to any singular moral vision. Thus we must take others' interests and values seriously in our moral deliberations.
2. While motives, principles, imperatives, and rules are useful instruments for moral deliberation, the balance of concern is on the consequences of our actions.
3. Only thorough inquiry – taking all moral experience seriously through the plurality of motives, means, and ends into account – before acting gives us the best chance of success in the face of an unknown future.

The preceding discussion of radical empiricism may seem, at this point at least, over-determined.[2] On the one hand, many have emphasized the importance of accepting that the dying process is part of our very acts of living, and while such a view of dying does imply some philosophical position, it need not be a "radical empiricism" that answers the call. On the other hand, the account given of radical empiricism implies much more than just the continuity of experience.

To demonstrate the unique aid that radical empiricism brings to our cause, we shall explore some implications of this attitude for bioethical theory and practice through recognition of what James calls "human blindness" and an investigation into how this "blindness" might be overcome in morally meaningful ways through a narrative account of socially situated selves. The emphasis on stories, of their authoring and reading, requires of physicians and patients an approach to medical encounters that takes up each others' life stories in morally imaginative ways that demonstrate an openness to the other's interests, values, and duties.[3]

---

[2] Of course, though possibly over-determined for this text, this account is, at best, a primer on radical empiricism. For a fuller account of radical empiricism and its metaphysical meliorist connections and consequences, see Wild 1980, Seigfried 1990, Brown 2000, and Talisse/Hester 2004, among many others.

[3] At this point, some might wish to see an account of how radical empiricism is an improvement over other views of the moral life – especially other pluralistic accounts of morality. This would take us even farther afield than the current philosophical groundwork of Chapters 2 and 3. I take the following accounts as making the case that moral pluralisms such as Rawlsian "reasonable pluralism" and Berlinian "value pluralism" fail, and that a pragmatic account of moral theory (based on radically empirical insights) succeeds. See Misak 2000 and Talisse 2000, 2004. In brief, Rawls (1996, and others like Rorty 1998) fails because without any metaphysics of experience, his account is too "thin" to hold up to scrutiny, and Berlin (1969, and others like Galston 2002) fails because he employs a comprehensive metaphysics of morals (liberalism) that violates his own insight that values are incommensurable, and therefore no one vision can be promoted. Pragmatism, and the radical empiricism that underlies it, accepts the Berlinian insight about a plurality of values, eschews one comprehensive vision of morality, and insists that inquiry is required to form the best solutions possible in the "tragic" finitude and realities of the moral life. See, for example, Hook 1974, 3–25.

Avoiding Our "Blindness"

My mother, Georgia Hansot, died recently in the intensive care unit of a major hospital in the eastern United States. She was 87 years old.... As I think back on it, I am astounded that I had so little inkling of how hard it would be to help my mother have the death she wanted.... An hour [after being admitted to the ICU], when I was allowed to see her, she was attached to a respirator and had a feeding tube inserted down her throat. What had happened... Exactly the opposite of what she had wished had occurred.... I found that I was dealing with a bewildering array of medical specialists trained to prolong lives, not to let their patients die.... My mother's wishes, as they were understood by her family physician and her daughter, were now subject to the approval of strangers: the cadre of cardiologists, neurologists, and pulmonologists who attend her. None of these specialists knew my mother, and they all had their convictions about how to do best for her.... The hospital came to feel like alien territory, full of medical strangers intent on maintaining my mother's vital signs at all costs. During her ordeal, my mother became increasingly frantic....

What is routine for hospital staff is all too often the first experience of its kind for critically ill patients and their families. (Elisabeth Hansot, quoted in Kaufman 2005, 22)

Some people like jazz; others do not. There are those who find pleasure in watching soap operas on television, while for others it has no appeal. These mark trivial differences, certainly, but differences nonetheless. Little hangs on these differences, but that does not mean that some minor irritations do not follow from them – for example, college students who watch soap operas at lunchtime in common areas of the dorm may not like the passerby who makes a snide comment; jazz aficionados struggle to find radio stations that will play their favorite music. However, the general understanding in the dorm may be that viewers of *All My Children* have reign over the TV from noon to 1 pm (at least they did in my dorm), and jazz fans still have CDs to pop into the car stereo if desired. As long as such accommodations can be made rather easily, all to the good.

It turns out, though, that other issues may cause deeper conflicts. Married couples may find their divergent interest seriously divisive. Those who are athletes may marry others who are uninterested in sports, and here significant conflict can arise. To pursue an interest in sports entails workouts, practice, travel, and game-time performance. For single people, without children, these activities might be easily seen as individual and personal, but for those married, a spouse's response to those activities and interests matter. Thus, expressed *dis*interest in athletics, bemusement over things seemingly vital to the activity, and cool reception to, say, hyper-enjoyment of a particular move or play can, at times, frustrate the relationship. Of course, should the roles be reversed concerning a deep interest of the spouse, the irritations, frustrations, and concerns run in the opposite direction.

Physicians and patients can talk past each other as well. Some patients, like Ms. Hansot, find their experiences intolerable; some value independent living; some just want to beat the odds. Patients envision living one way, dying another. Physicians come in all stripes, too – aiming at cure, aiming at alleviating suffering, aiming at concession. Specialists and sub-specialists bring focus and determination as much as caring and compassion. Many of these values and attitudes are compatible, but not always. In fact, some may be all-consuming for those who hold them; others may have flexibility of vision, taking them beyond their own immediate concerns.

James notes that our values routinely affect our forms of judgment, and he calls this the "blindness" of our human condition. He observes:

We are practical beings, each of us with limited functions and duties to perform. Each is bound to feel intensely the importance of his own duties and the significance of the situations that call these forth. But this feeling is in each of us a vital secret, for sympathy with which we vainly look to others. The others are too much absorbed in their own vital secrets to take an interest in ours. Hence the stupidity and injustice of our opinions, so far as they deal with the significance of alien lives. Hence the falsity of our judgments, so far as they presume to decide in an absolute way on the value of other persons' conditions or ideals. (James [1899a], 629–630)

James speaks here of the blindness of human beings to each others' duties, interests, and values – a blindness brought on by self-absorption in our own interests and values. He warns of the problems that arise from making "absolute" judgments concerning others, given this blindness in us. If we take James seriously, then we must be careful in our attempts to decide for other people concerning situations that affect them. Our self-concerned habits lead to the easy judgment that what is best for others is simply what we judge to be best for ourselves; at which point, we simply adjudicate according to our own obligations and satisfactions rather than attempt to understand other people's desires and beliefs.

The moral implications are obvious, and it is not unimportant to note, in the context of the larger project of this book, that these implications are particularly relevant and decidedly important in medical encounters where, because of biological forces of injury or disease, we turn to physicians in order to gain some control over our lives and bodies. But of course, if "blindness" to others' interests, values, and duties afflicts us all, it would seem especially worth noting in the relationship between physicians and patients, where communication about personal ends and development of common ends are keys to a positive outcome for all concerned. The physician will attempt during the course of the relationship to fulfill her duty of healing as it is defined by her personal and professional values, while the patient will try to return to living healthily. Without relinquishing the necessary knowledge and abilities that empower physicians in their chosen profession, some authoritative control must be relinquished by physicians in order to overcome the "blindness" dangerously apparent in many medical interactions. Control and "blindness" hinder a patient's ability to participate actively in her own healing process, thus said blindness must be recognized, and where possible, overcome.

By employing a radically empirical attitude, we attempt to see the world through the eyes of others, to attempt to understand, not just the expressed interests they have, but the very fount of those interests.

Self as Social Product[4]

James's desire to overcome blindness arises from the need to understand our fellow human beings. But such a "need" rests firmly on the

---

4 The following section is adapted from Hester 2001.

belief that we are all in this together. That is, my interest and beliefs, as they manifest themselves in my behaviors and chosen actions, do not reside in isolation for those around me. I, in fact, do affect others, and vice versa. However, the claim, at this level, is merely prudential. The mere fact that my actions do affect others is not sufficient to explain why I should *care* that my actions do affect others. That is, there is nothing in James's argument, other than fear of judging incorrectly, that explains the need to overcome blindness. So far, then, we lack, a clear grounding for this morally charged claim. To build up such grounding, I begin with an observation from Cheryl Misak.

> It of course remains true that I cannot get under your skin and feel what you feel from the inside, as it were. So, in a sense I cannot fully comprehend your experiences. But I comprehend enough, something which is shown by the fact that I can speak to you about them, interpret what you say or write about them, and learn something about what it is that you feel. [. . . L]anguage and communication are public: The fact that we communicate, interpret and translate shows that we share a tremendous amount. (Misak 2000, 134)

Language demonstrates that we are not isolated and insular beings. Communication implicates others, and it implies something about ourselves – that, we are social beings. Philosopher George Herbert Mead's account of human beings as socially constituted demonstrates precisely what Misak observes but that James's own position never flushed out – that the social nature of the human animal entails that each individual's actions be part and parcel of the communities in which she lives, and thus as products of society we are always-already moral beings who (ought to) take account of each other.

Mead's account of the social nature of the "self" begins as a story of human development. While biological, physiological beings are *uniquely* situated, no organic mass should be mistaken for a "self"; it takes social processes to creaste an individualized "self." So we see that the newborn makes no immediate distinctions between her body or needs and the movements of the environment of which she is a part. The thumb is not *her* thumb; it is an object. It *appears*; then it *satisfies*. In this way, the child *undergoes* experience but does not comprehend or control it. Over time, however, children creatively separate the actions of others from their own. Rather than merely parroting others, toddlers look for responses from others to their own actions. Simple actions elicit responses, and the act of communicating – language – ultimately becomes the shared means of signification. The child says "bottle" in anticipation of the response by the parent to give the nippled object to her. But in saying "bottle," the child reacts to the object (if only internally) as she expects the parent to react. She leans towards it, reaches for it. The infant even becomes as much a member of the audience as the parents do, listening to her*self.*

The self arises, then, in "self-conscious" behavior. Each individual begins to react to itself with expectation, and those expectations come from experience with how *others* react to what we do and say. That is, we develop as individuals in and through an awareness of the attitudes of others; we take on the attitude of the community itself. As Mead explains, every action "comes within a given social group or community to stand for a particular act or response, namely, the act or response which it calls forth explicitly in the individual who makes it" (Mead 1962, 47). Community, then, is constitutive of and prior to the self. "It cannot be said that the individuals come first and the community later, for the individuals arise in the very process [of living] itself" (Mead 1962, 189).

The key for our account is therefore that organization of the self has important moral consequences, for meaningful action must recognize and respond to others as we take on their attitudes as our own. And the meaning of our actions comes not by way of our intentions (though they may arise from our own impulses) but in how they are taken by others – that is, how they bear out in their consequences.

If we look now towards the end of the action rather than toward the impulse itself, we find that those ends are good which lead to the realization of the self as a social being. *Our morality gathers about our social conduct. It is as social beings that we are moral beings.* On the one side stands the society which makes the self possible, and on the other side stands the self that makes a highly organized society possible. The two answer to each other in moral conduct. (Mead 1962, 386 [emphasis mine])

Moral conduct and judgments are social. "We are all of us in some sense changing the social order in which we belong; our very living does it, and we ourselves change as we go.... That process of continuing reconstruction is the process of value, and the only

essential imperative I can see is that this essential social process has
to go on" (Mead 1938, 460). Mead's self-and-community reciprocity
leads to his "essential imperative," which can be restated in ethical
terms: "One can never [judge] simply from his own point of view.
We have to look at it from the point of view of a social situation.... The
only rule that an ethics can present is that an individual should rationally [and imaginatively] deal with all the values that are found in
a specific problem." (Mead 1962, 387–388 [emphasis mine]) Since
my activities are, in part, products of the social conditions in which
I find myself, and will consequently affect others of my social group,
I must account for the many (and often competing) interests at play
in the situation. Those interests arise from other selves who are part
of the environment in which I wish to exercise my own (communally
constituted) desires.

The social psychology of Mead, then, leads to ethical insights that
ground the radically empirical need to overcome human blindness.
Humans as socially situated "selves" are substantially determined in
relationship to the communities of which they are a part. As such, our
individual interests both speak to and have consequences for those
communities. Mead's ethical message is that none of our values can
claim *a priori* primacy; instead, we must try first to account for all the
interests involved before determining the morality of our proposed
actions. As we will see in the next chapter with James's account of
de facto and moral obligations, this is the basic moral expression of
radical empiricism itself. Again, Mead: "In the solution of the [moral]
problem we must take all relevant values into account.... [I]n the
problems in which values come in conflict with one another, we want
to reconstruct our lives so as to take in all the values involved" (Mead
1938, 461).

But a question lingers: How might we "deal with all the values
found in a specific problem"?

Narrative and the Social Self[5]

Values seem to be expressed everywhere, and gathering them up
for consideration is no easy task. However, as we share language, we

---

[5] The following section is adapted from Hester 2001.

express values, communicating them to each other. It is a process that, as Steven Fesmire (1995; 2003) explains, involves an imaginative projection of others' attitudes and interests in our communications, and that projection shapes our very selves. This projection is often a "story-structured" capacity that guides our conduct and develops our selves. This "story-structured" process, or "narrative," is morally significant, for the social self is an ethical self, and as Fesmire explains, "moral behavior is intelligible only in the setting of a life-narrative, which of course interplays with other life-narratives" (Fesmire 2003, 79).

Selves are constructs built, in part, through the comings and goings within a community. One way to understand these interactions of selves is through narrative accounts. We can and do construct and use stories to make sense of our experiences, and this use of stories can be valuable to investigate.[6]

First, narratives do not begin from nothing. They start where we are now, using both past and present situations.[7] We weave a story that, in part, takes account of certain "facts" of life. These facts are interpretations of events involving people, places, and things. In their very use, these facts are considered "relevant," and "relevant" facts are choices made by individuals revealing how and where they stand now. In this way, narratives are purposive. They are told for some reason(s). Stories about ourselves and others weave the pieces of experience into a complex fabric. Thus, stories do more than

---

[6] It is important to make clear that I am using narratives and stories in a functional, not foundational, way. That is, I am not arguing that narratives are *the* mode in which selves come to be or that they are the *basis* of morality (cf. Chambers 1999; Walker 1998; Brody 2003). I am, however, arguing that understanding the functionality of narratives can *help* us gain perspective on how selves come to be and can be *useful* (i.e., instrumental) in working through moral dilemmas. Hilde Nelson has argued that the use of narrative in ethics can be segregated into five categories: reading stories, telling stories, comparing stories, literary analysis of stories, and invoking stories (Nelson 1997, x–xii). All of these can help in better understanding the ethical aspects of experience. In what follows, however, I concentrate on the first three categories. For excellent discussions of several perspectives on the use of narratives in bioethics, see the essays in Nelson 1997. For a comprehensive take on narrative concerns in medical practice, see Brody 1987/2003; Charon 2006.

[7] Surely there can be times of so-called "discontinuity" where "epiphany" or "revelation" or "radical transformation" in, through, or of narratives occurs. But even these moments do not begin from a formless void; instead they are reworkings of elements that already exist in experience with elements new to the situation.

recount the past or explain the present; they also project into the future. Personal and social narratives are taken up into experience, which is itself future-directed. Imaginative projection places history into the context of the ever-evolving self and the constantly changing community environment. And yet stories are not simply logical reconstruction – they follow their own flow as much as they do the intentions of the author, and while they help order the quasi-chaos of the world, they are "ever not quite" – they never capture and order the world completely. That is, they remain underdetermined, perspectival, and limited.

Further, our stories are made not simply in our tellings but through our activities. When asked to explain who we are, we speak, and when attempting to express who we are, we simply act. We are not merely storytellers but narrative actors. We enact the stories that are our lives in the very processes of living. Narratives are a means by which we create meaning for ourselves and our world.

Narrative employs language that, we have already stated, is constitutively communal. Language is never simply mine alone; even in introspective moments, I "talk" to myself using the language given to me by the community through which I have become acculturated. Language is shared. Narrative, then, employs this shared language in order to weave new patterns out of and into old. It takes available subject matter and attempts to make a coherent account of it for oneself or another. As J. M. Bernstein writes:

One of the ways human beings assess and interpret the events of their life [*sic*] is through the *construction of plausible narratives*. Narratives represent events not as general laws but rather as elements of a history where a continuing individual or collective subject suffers or brings about dramatic, i.e. meaningful, changes. A change is meaningful in relation to past *and future events*. (Bernstein 1990, 55 [emphasis mine])

Narratives arise from something; they are moments of choosing "relevant" facts that paint a new picture. However, narratives go further, making these "facts" "meaningful" by directing them toward "future events." That is, purpose infuses the story, shaping its content and form. This is a *genuinely creative moment*. "The telling does not merely expose or report that which exists prior to narrating. It produces it"

(Charon 2006, 45). A story is "constructed" in order to make sense of lived experience. This "making" is artistic.

But authors are themselves moral creatures, value-laden, and the creation of stories implicates the creator, not just the subject-matter. So, John Hardwig correctly points out that storytelling cuts both ways, for we not only tell stories about ourselves but about others as well. (Hardwig 1997a) "Biography," then, and not just "autobiography," raises very important questions concerning who is telling the story and what her own position, powers, and motives are. For example, in the medical setting, is it the patient or physician who is telling the story? And is the story being told about the patient, medicine, the physician, what? How does the story differ when the patient tells a story about herself and when the physician tells a story about the patient?

Arthur Frank illustrates the problem of "authorship" through his own personal illness experience:

> ... I began to realize that ... any sense that was to be made of my experience was going to have to come from me. They [the physicians] were telling the story of my illness, but this story was not my experience, and if I was not to lose the experience that was mine, and lose part of myself with it, I needed to tell my own story. (Frank 1997, 32)

Personal stories, for Frank, empower the teller, taking back experience that might otherwise be lost. However, it is clear that we must not only tell our stories but tell stories about one another. Physicians *must* "re-tell" the story of the patient in the context of the physician's own practices. As Robert Coles's mentor reminds us, "The people who come to see us [physicians] bring their stories. ... They hope we know how to interpret their stories correctly. We have to remember that what we hear is their story." (Coles 1989, 7) But Frank turns this around as well: "The ill person should realize that physicians, whatever their intentions, have a different job description and take their stories from different communities." (Frank 1997, 45)

Further, Frank's comments imply and caution that the development of narratives engages an audience. The hearer, reader, or interpreter of the story (be it spoken, written, or enacted) is also part of this creative process. Communication that occurs between and among individuals takes both careful crafting, on the one hand, and sensitive, generous, imaginative interpretation, on the other. Herein lies one of the great strengths and weaknesses of a narrative approach. While stories paint pictures that create novel insight, they are subject to interpretation and investigation from all members of the community for and in which they are told. Becoming a good interpreter, however, can take hard work to mold "literarily" sensitive habits. As Brody points out, "Inevitably, a sickness story told by physicians for a medical purpose will be quite different from the story told by the patient of the illness as experienced" (Brody 2003, 10). So it is no offhand moral point that "interpretation" matters, for the generous interpreter is herself *responsible* for the re-telling of the story (if only to herself).

In medical encounters, these narrative insights require that both physicians and patients not only become good "writers" but "readers." They must become interpreters who filter stories through the ongoing cultural/personal narrative of the reader in order to make them fit within the reader's own framework. Both physicians and patients must work on their skills of literary interpretation "in the special way a story requires" (Coles 1989, 23). However, they must enhance their abilities to fit stories together, *without doing great violence to the accounts given by others.* This is no simple skill easily cultivated. It takes practice to create such intelligent habits.

Of course, as Tristram Engelhardt correctly points out, there is an asymmetry in the healing relationship that, if unrecognized, may stifle positive narrative exchange:

Patients, when they come to see a health care professional, are in unfamiliar territory. They enter a terrain of issues that has been carefully defined through the long history of the health care professions. A patient is unlikely to present for care with as well-analyzed and considered judgments as those possessed by health care professionals. Professionals have a community of colleagues to reinforce their views and to sustain them in their recommendations. In addition, the interchange of health care professional and patient is defined by the language of health care. Pains, disabilities, and even fears are translated into the special jargon of the health care professions. (Engelhardt 1986, 256)

To be a patient, as Richard Zaner has noted, is to be in a compromised position of *having* to trust the physician, whereas to be a physician is to have the history, technology, and language of the institution of medicine supporting your position of power (cf. Zaner 1988). Thus, power within institutions of medicine in which patients find themselves when at their most compromised is in the hands of their caregivers, and the danger of having their stories co-opted in the face of this asymmetrical medical encounter, as Frank pointed out earlier, is ever-present.

Therefore the physician is charged with the greater moral burden in many instances. "Physicians should not simply assume that the medical story is the patient's story or that no negotiation between the two stories is needed for the patient to receive the full benefit of the medical work" (Brody 2003, 10). She must work to provide a space for the patient's story in the patient's own language. The physician must also work to develop a story of medicine and of the particular encounter in which the patient can find herself, in order to "honor the meanings of her patients' narratives of illness" (Charon 2006, 3). Meanwhile, the patient should strive to develop the medical story for herself – accounting for her life, and including her desires and interests.

But for the patient to find that voice it often takes a physician who is sensitive both to people and to narrative, and not simply a physician who is technically competent. In turn, this implies that physicians must be well trained not only in the biomedical sciences but in human, social affairs. I take it that this is what Edmund Pellegrino has in mind at the end of his article "The Anatomy of Clinical Judgments," when he calls for humanities education in medical school:

If medicine is a science, and art . . . , medical students will need a more explicit education in the non-scientific components of clinical judgment. . . . The liberal arts, and the humanities, . . . need vigorous refurbishment in medical education where it will become more obvious to the student that he *needs* the liberal attitude of mind to function fully as a physician. (Pellegrino 1979, 191–192)

Still further, however, my discussion implies that physicians and patients both must work through morally imaginative deliberations to include as many interests as possible of those involved or related to the encounter. No simple principled approach will do, nor will straightforward technical competence. We must be artists, creatively invoking technology and scientific knowledge in the stories of people – that is, selves in community and acculturated. We must account for their interest as related in their stories in order to use technical abilities in successful ways. Dewey states:

What is relied upon is personal contact and communication; while personal attitudes, going deeper than the mere asking of questions, are needed in order to establish the confidence which is a condition for the patient's telling the story of his past....[O]rganic modification is there – it is indispensable.... But this is not enough. The physical fact has to be taken up into the context of personal relations between human being and human being before it becomes a fact of the living present. (1991 [1939b], 334)

It is the patient's "telling the story" of herself that must be taken into account by the physician. This accounting must then be sensitive to "personal relations between human being and human being" in order to fashion a truly moral solution. In this way, the physician is an artist whenever she moves away from general principles, and instead is attentive to the individual patient and her story. Whenever the physician works to read the story of the patient as a socially situated human being in the writing of the medical encounter, there the physician is artistic. Again, Dewey:

Just in the degree in which a physician is an artist in his work he uses his science, no matter how extensive and accurate, to furnish him with tools of inquiry into the individual case, and with methods of forecasting a method of dealing with it. Just in degree in which, no matter how great his learning, he subordinates the individual case to some classification of diseases and some generic rule of treatment, he sinks to the level of the routine mechanic. His intelligence and his action become rigid, dogmatic, instead of free and flexible. (1988 [1920], 176)

The "dogmatic" physician loses sight of narrative and moral imagination and replaces this with "routine mechanics." Though our scientific knowledge is general, every case is different. The art is in the coupling of the general with the individual patient. To do this, the physician and patient can both attend to the details of human living as expressed through the stories they tell, and in this way they take on the radically empirical attitude of taking each others' experiences seriously while developing their stories. In fact, as Frank has put it quite strongly, "Our moral practices are our stories" (Frank 1997, 39).

Beyond Narrative

So we can now respond to the concern, raised by the ethical barrier of our human "blindness," for a way to understand not just the expressed interests others have, but whence those interests arise. Socially situated selves have a narrative character to their actions, developed in their life stories and expressed interests. Investigation into those stories not only elucidates the grounding of those interests but also illustrates and feeds the communal aspects of individuality, connecting us with others.

We are, simply put, individuals – in-community-with-others – and these social relationships shape the very selves we are. Such an account has been called "communitarian" and has been subsequently criticized on the grounds that it runs the risk of subsuming individual interest to those of the community. However, I take the position to be a pragmatic, not communitarian, account and, as such, I have already argued that cultivating sensitivity to understanding personal stories of and by individuals gives credit not only to their unique individualities but also to the communities and cultures in which those individualities arise. In fact, narrative investigation, by offering a way out of our human blindness towards others' feelings and insights, interests, and values, offers a way out of communitarian sublimation. It takes the socially situated nature of the individual seriously while paying strict attention to *individuality*.

In the final part of this chapter, I shall take radical empiricism a step further, showing that we bring *meaning* to our lives through the stories we *enact*, and in particular, the descriptive/creative interplay in stories that gives them meaning. That is, the very *meanings* of our life-stories are to be found in our communal *and* individual – or better yet, communally individual – experiences coupled with the imaginative projections we extrapolate from those experiences. We are "meaning" seekers. Through our daily activities and life plans, we work to give purpose to our existences. And this is no less true (and maybe even more importantly noted) for the lives of patients who find themselves in the midst of their personal experiences of illness, and thereby to patients who live in and through diseases, injuries, afflictions, and their corresponding concerns at the end of life.

Meaningful Living: Personal Significance in Community[8]

[Paddy Esposito] was thirty years of age, tall, extremely thin, dressed almost always in a dark blue corduroy suit with a small red flower in the buttonhole (he said that was to celebrate, because "every day is a good day"), bearded and fierce-looking, but with an infectious smile ready in an instant to breakout upon his large, expressive lips and in his soft brown eyes.... He was single, but had a large circle of friends. Paddy suffered from a mysterious progressive inflammatory disease (myocarditis) that attacked the smooth muscle of his heart. He was always short of breath. But many people commented that this was one of the least remarkable things about him. Although he had a serious incapacity [from which he would eventually die]... he made remarkably little of it....

He was also a man of great inner peace and... real wisdom. Paddy had dropped out of law school after his second year, soon after the diagnosis of myocarditis was made.... Before his illness he had been, by his own admission, restless, immensely ambitious, egotistical. After [traveling the globe], his health was much worse, but in his felicitous words, "I was so much better."

He decided his role in life was to serve others, to bring them the peace and wisdom he had found. (Kleinman 1988, 140–141)

Patients are never just "patients," never just passive receptors. As humans they actively pursue meaningful lives. But their illnesses and injuries can thwart their efforts, requiring simple readjustments or cataclysmic redefinition of the meaning of their actions, pursuits, and purposes. Recalling James's radically empirical meliorism (the idea that we have a hand in the development of truth in the world – which results directly from holding a radically empirical attitude towards life), meaning is for us to make, not simply to find. The significance of our lives may in fact be waiting on us and our efforts in order to come into being. One way to describe this "meliorism" of

[8] The following section is adapted from Hester 2001.

meaning in a personal fashion is to say that I create meaning in my life every time I couple some personally and intelligently conceived goal or ideal with the courage and labor necessary to achieve it. The ideals that I have, express, and pursue come in a vocabulary that is not mine alone; it is a social vocabulary – physicians need the medical language, philosophers need metaphysical language, and so forth. And, as argued already, though individualized as "my" ideals, the process is communal and common to us all.

But ideals alone are not meaningful in themselves. Those socially situated, but individually conceived ideals come to life and gain significance through intelligence and fortitude.

The significance of life . . . . . . is the offspring of a marriage of two different parents, either of whom alone are barren. The ideals taken by themselves give no reality, the virtues by themselves no novelty. . . . [T]he thing of deepest – or at any rate, of comparatively deepest – significance in life does seem to be its character of *progress*, or that strange union of reality with ideal novelty which it continues from one moment to another to present. (James [1899b], 657)[9]

An individual progresses in life whenever she is able to develop an end and deploy means to attain it within her lived experience. For example, the desire to walk in a patient with a spinal cord injury gives meaning to her life as she progresses through medical treatment and physical therapy. The activity is meaningful precisely because it entails a personal ideal (wanting to walk) and the wherewithal to achieve the ideal (the strength of character to succeed that energizes the hours of effort).

---

[9] James does qualify this idea of "significance" employed here with the phrase "for communicable and publicly recognizable purposes." I believe this qualification is made to contrast with remarks he makes elsewhere in such works as *The Varieties of Religious Experience*, where he admits to the possibility of a kind of mystical "private" significance in an individual's life. Cf. James 1902, 379–429, Lectures XVI & XVII, "Mysticism." In particular, James's qualifier specifically opposes his use of the term "mystical states of consciousness" in *Varieties*, where he begins his definition of this term with the idea that the mystical is "ineffable," "transient," and "passive" – three terms not readily applicable to socially recognizable meaning in life. Since my discussion is concerned with lived, social experience, James's qualifier becomes unnecessarily redundant.

Of course, simpler, less time-consuming, more routine ideals and labors (such as desiring to eat and then preparing a meal) are in their own ways instances of meaningful progress, for it is our everyday labors that develop the character of our grander schemes, whereas grander schemes help to shape the development of everyday pursuits. Our daily ideals often become part of the means to yet further ideals, and still are themselves ends to be enjoyed without recourse to their function in our higher goals. Again, physical therapy, for example, takes many individual efforts that come together to produce a self-supporting individual, and each activity – for example, using support bars, weight training, the first ten feet of distance traveled – can be satisfying and enjoyable in its own right quite independent of the connections to the whole.

Given this two-part account of "meaning," every person at any stage of life can have ideals, and meaning in life is highly individualized. As James says, "[T]here is nothing absolutely ideal: ideals are relative to the lives that entertain them" (James [1899b], 656). Here again, we are confronted with James's own radically empirical attitude. Experience everywhere and anywhere is taken seriously, and "meaning," in this way, arises from individual and specific ideals held. Thus, for James, there is no *a priori*, overarching meaning to life; there is only the concrete character of radical empiricism manifest in the particular instances of meaning created by a particular person in the full context of her life. Of course, we must remember that this is a two-part account. Having ideals alone does not make life meaningful. James's account is processive, and this process of meaning *begins* when the "novelty" of an "intellectually conceived" goal takes hold of the attention. However, those ideals gain their significance when they call available habits and abilities into action. Let us take a moment, then, to discuss the "parental" relationship between ideals and fortitude in order to better understand their "offspring" (meaningful activity).

Ideals that are worthy of pursuit, James states, must be both "intellectually conceived" and have "novelty at least for him whom the ideal grasps." That is, ideals must reside in reflective consciousness and take hold of individuals uniquely. "Novelty" denotes this quality of uniqueness exemplified by possible ends as they are experienced by an individual. Ideals that "grasp" an individual take hold of her attention and move her to action. The idealizer finds in the ideal the possibility for unique expression of her talents. And even though some goals may seem mundane to others, for the person who is "grasped," a sense of engagement is felt where an individual's abilities and creativity are called forth. "Sodden routine is incompatible with ideality, although *what is sodden routine for one person may be ideal novelty for another*" (James [1899b], 656 [emphasis mine]). The ideal itself is further shaped by a person's individualized approach to it. Take almost any example of someone's expressed interest – for example, interest in medicine, love of jazz, enjoyment of philosophy. For you or me, there may be no great novelty in studying biochemistry, listening to Muzak, reading about transcendental meditation, but it is no great news to us that others do enjoy these activities, finding in them a venue to exercise talents, enliven their aural world, or gain insight into the human condition. Furthermore, there can be moments of historic novelty when particular individuals idealize for an entire epoch (becoming "ideals" themselves) – for example, the greatness of William Osler, the genius of John Coltrane, the intellect of Aristotle. More common, however, are the daily engagements by any one of us as we pursue our desirable ends as we study, play, listen, read, practice.

"Intellectually conceived," on the other hand, takes us beyond mere novelty; it signifies the need, *before pursuit*, for reflection upon our ends in light of means available. *This is the all-important requirement of inquiry.* James, again, fails us here, lacking, as he does, as account of inquiry. But fortunately we have done some of this work already with the development of narrative understandings of selves. Accordingly, intelligent ideals can be well described as those that arise from the fusion of the descriptive/creative function of an acceptable, coherent story; they "fit" within the means available and other ends that have been put forth in the situation.

Another way to understand the process of intelligence comes from John Dewey's account of the continuum between means and ends, and his distinction between *de facto* and *de jure* qualities. On the latter, Dewey reminds us that in pursuing ends (ideals), the value of any end attained "is a value of something which in being an end, an outcome, stands in relation to the means of which it is the consequence. Hence, if the object in question is prized *as* an end of 'final' value [if it is meaningful], it is valued *in this relation*" (1991 [1939a], 227). To put this in another way, reflection takes mere valu*ed* objects – aka, descriptively, what we like – and makes them valu*able* – that is, creatively, what we should pursue. Intelligently conceived ideals are not simply something (*de facto*) desir*ed* as ends in themselves, but are determined to be (*de jure*) desir*able* upon investigation of costs and consequences; they gain *warrant* as a result of reflection. They are, therefore, *worthy of our desire and our efforts*. This use of intelligence is what situates personal goals into the complex of the communal environment in which the goals arise and are to be played out. In other words, this process, where ideals are scrutinized by inquiry to determine whether or not they should be realized, is an acknowledgment that it is the narrative, *socially* situated self that makes ideals meaningful, for it is the process of inquiry – intelligent, creative, and radically empirical in its sensitivity to others' interests – that produces significance in life.

For example, a physician may wish to order a battery of tests, but the desire alone is not enough to make it worthy of pursuit. She must investigate the concerns raised by the expressed symptoms, the interests of the patient and others affected by the decision, economic factors, availability, time constraints, and so on. Only after having followed out this inquiry can she move from a mere "whimsical" ideal to something that is determined to be either valuable or not. "Whimsical" desires without reflection, no matter how much they capture the attention, rarely come to fruition, and when they do, make for the possibility of unforeseen conflict down the line. Intelligence helps us sort through (or better yet, intelligence is the sorting through of) various ends-in-view and the means available to achieve them in order to determine those "worth the effort."

These requirements of "novelty" and "intelligence" imply that ideals do not reside beyond experience as formal or absolute ends; they are created within and by our daily lives. That is, they arise out of our ongoing stories as well as the stories of those with whom we come in contact. As both intellectually conceived and novel, ideals must touch us and come to fruition in our experiences, employing means available *and* accounting for others' ends as well. Admittedly, "[T]aken nakedly, abstractly, and immediately, you see that mere ideals are the cheapest things in life. Everybody has them in some shape or other, personal or general, sound or mistaken, low or high." (James [1899b], 657) However, significance in life cannot stop with "cheap" ideals. These often lead to frustration and failure. The immature have no depth in thought or act.

So James insists that the means employed are of equal importance to the ends, and the means also arise out of our experiences, our life stories. An ideal must be not only immediately and abstractly desired but also wedded to the discipline and courage needed to pursue it. If personal ends are to become fulfilled (within experience), we must back our "ideal visions with what the laborers have, the sterner stuff of . . . virtue; we must multiply [the ideals'] sentimental surface by the dimension of the active will, if we are to have *depth*, if we are to have anything cubical and solid in the way of character." (James [1899b], 657) Again, we see that a continuum of means and ends exists such that the means employed give otherwise empty, flighty ideals content and character. Significance, then, comes from this active striving to actualize our personal goals.

To restate, "significance" develops from a fusion of personal, particular ideals with courage, strength, and intelligence – that is, the virtues that drive people to embody these ideals in their daily lives. James's term for this is 'progress,' and progress incorporates the intellectual ability to create goals and the actional fortitude to fulfill them, regardless of our current location on the timeline between birth and death. Also, whereas fortitude and strength are sometimes difficult to muster, ideals arise everywhere; they are part and parcel of our daily lives; they are "the cheapest things in life."[10]

---

[10] We would be wise to cultivate the ability, particularly as we become elderly and our means are reduced in number and potency, to find meaning more and more in those activities that youth affords us the luxury of ignoring. Rather than shaping meaning through the development of long-term goals and activities, as we age and move closer to dying (though I do not wish to restrict this only to the elderly), we should attempt to develop significance out of the more immediate pleasures and basic activities of life. As we find our abilities change, our goals must also. The less stamina and strength we demonstrate, wisdom tells us, the more immediate our ends should become. The sounds of the day, the taste of the food, the movements

Meaningful living, then, is highly individualized, but always with communal content – articulated in a shared language and our narratives. Ideals themselves arise from our experiences in and of our communities and environments. And our intellectual support and courageous activities in pursuit of our ideals both take into account and come home to rest in this actual lived experience. In this way, it should be clear that meaning is not merely "voluntary" and "subjective." As I have argued throughout my account of narrative significance, the stories we tell, and the meanings they convey, arise from and feed back into the community. They are open for approval, disapproval, consternation, disagreement, reconstruction, and/or acceptance by ourselves and others. In this way, they are, or become, as "objective" as can be. They are objective because, in the words of Sidney Hook, they are "warranted" (1974, 65). So, as the result of and open to further social investigation and evaluation, the meanings of our narratives are themselves part of the moral fabric of experience.

In the next chapter, we will confront directly the moral fabric of experience that arises in end-of-life considerations, and we will take the last step in this philosophical argument in order to demonstrate the direct implications of the radically empirical attitude with regard to concerns at the end of life.

> of the body, all can be sources of meaning. If sight begins to degenerate, simply hearing the song of a bird can be an activity both idealized and appreciated. When a hot day diminishes energy, the sensation of flavorful ice cream flowing coolly down the throat can reinvigorate. As muscles begin to weaken, the swinging of the legs and arms in everyday walking can prove defiant against the aging process. In this way, we can retain meaning throughout life by pursuing ends appropriate to our means.

3

Radical Experience and Tragic Duty

Moral Dying

There are times when a man ought to be more afraid of living than dying.

F. J. E. Woodbridge

[T]here are situations in which, because of the conditions of survival, the worst thing we can know of anyone is that he has survived.

Sidney Hook

The account of "meaning" and "significance" given in Chapter 2 was, it should be clear, a restatement under a different guise of radical empiricism itself – that is, "meaningful living" is another name for radically empirical, reflective narrative. Since meaning develops from the operations of intelligent deliberation upon individualized ideals, what comes next in our account of the moral implications of radical empiricism is a discussion of moral deliberation that can move from the level of particularity to the more "universal" (and back). To do so, the discussion that follows turns to a more traditional ethical language, one that takes us from the existence of personal desires (one form of idealizing) to the requirements of moral obligations (what follows for ourselves and others when desires are deemed worthy of pursuit). Again, even with this turn to a more traditional moral language or "obligations," what follows is yet another restatement of our radically empirical account of meaning that will also demonstrate how moral deliberation on end-of-life issues arises from the specific situations of dying persons while employing concepts and methods that make decisions around the end of life ethical.

The account begins openly within traditional moral philosophy – the language of "duties" and "obligations"; but whereas these moral terms have historically been developed through rational, ideal, *a priori* frameworks, I wish to reconstruct them as arising out of, not prior to, experience. This will then allow us to take up the first substantive end-of-life issue in the book – a radically empirical answer to the question of whether or not there exists a "duty to die."

Grounding "Obligations"[1]

Moral concepts of *duties, obligations, normativity, imperatives* fill the pages of philosophy/ethics texts, particularly since the beginning of the so-called modern period of Western culture. Whether we are under the obligations of a "social contract" or rationally required to follow a categorical imperative, many philosophical figures – be they John Locke, Immanuel Kant, or John Rawls – argue that ethical activity must be based on following the rules of conduct, protecting human rights, or doing one's moral duty.

Of course, lived experience is often more complex and difficult than much of ethical theory would suggest. Decisions we confront everyday have their overt and covert ethical components, and the formulas suggested by ethicists rarely come into play. Shall we go out to eat with friends or stay at home and save money? Should we save all our spare money or give to charity? Must we give to charity or help our friends and family? Ethical theory rarely comes to mind when weighing our options, trying to answer these and similar questions. Quite simply, we "muddle through."

Bioethics, as a sub-discipline of ethics, attempts to do on paper and in the hospital what we rarely do in daily practice – bring to bear ethical theory on specific problems of lived experience. Bioethicists

---

[1] The following is adapted from a presentation I gave at the annual conference of the Society for the Advancement of American Philosophy, March 2001 (that talk was later reprinted in *Streams of William James*, v1, n3:13–16).

reformulate the great thoughts of philosophers and others in order to bring insight to moral questions in the field of medicine and related human endeavors. What can we take from John Stuart Mill in order to help with organ resource allocation? How might Aristotle's ethical theory inform us in relationships between physicians and patients?

This chapter will focus on issues at the end of life that present moral concerns for those who, for reasons of disease, injury, or basic degeneration, find themselves contemplating their deaths. Confronted with strains on relationships, activities, and economics, it is not unreasonable for some to contemplate the question of whether, at a certain point, living actually poses a moral problem and therefore whether there might be an actual *duty* to die. Is it the case that some (if not all) people who are nearing the ends of their lives are at some point in the process obligated to die? Can there ever be such a duty? To answer these questions, I begin by elucidating the moral concept of "duty" in a way that differs from most traditional philosophical accounts.

Whence Cometh Our Duties

The concept of "duty" has a long and varied history in ethics, and it is best to establish the sense in which it will be used here. Most of us are familiar with the traditional view of moral duty. "Duty," it has been said, has primacy in the moral life. While we may always wish that our actions produce good outcomes for almost everyone involved, outcomes can rarely be guaranteed. However, as moral creatures, we do have and can follow through with the obligations we have to others. Such obligations, it is argued, arise as part-and-parcel of being rational creatures. Immanuel Kant, for example, argued that there was in fact only one moral duty, because reason could dictate only one rule to follow – act in a way that you would be willing to allow others to act in similar circumstances. Kant's imperative, then, is decidedly "universal." However, unlike Kant, the meaning of "duty" that I will employ will not be driven by a primary concern for universalizing in moral thinking – that is, I do not begin from some categorical/rational imperative that orders all moral deliberation.² Of course, Kant is not the only philosopher to give primacy to duty-following, but the moral tradition of which he is a clear example is one that has attempted to develop, *a priori*, the rules of morality that we must follow. In bioethics, duty-based ethics finds voice through the ten moral rules of Bernard Gert (2004), and even the "common morality" claims not only of Gert but of Tom Beauchamp and James Childress (2009) as well. These theories claim that there simply are common moral norms that are inherent in any account of the moral life, and as Gert clearly explains, those norms are rational, identifiable, and universal.

My point here is not to give an account of deontological (duty-based) ethics, but simply to show that such theories traditionally place a premium on the concept of duty as not just *a* moral concept but *the* moral concept. It makes "duty" *fundamental*, not, as I will argue, *instrumental*. Alternatively, though, my contention is that "duty," in this *strong* sense, does not exhaust the moral life; it cannot be the exclusive concept for moral deliberation. And yet the account to be given does find its grounding in a universal human experience – the experience of having desires that demand satisfaction.

Related to the deontological approach there are so-called rights theorists who also speak of duties, though it is probably best to call them "obligations" so as not to confuse them with the deontologists' concept. According to these theorists, obligations are intimately related to rights – specifically, where there is a right, there comes a corresponding obligation. The relationship between rights and obligations is thereby correlative. Of course, with such theories, everything depends on what counts as a right, and thus what follows as obligations we have. Are there "inalienable" rights, basic "natural" rights, only legal rights, what? If we identify a right, are we obligated to see that right come to fruition or only obligated to keep from interfering with its exercise by others? These are questions long debated, and while important, this book is not the medium

---

² In fact, for the devout Kantian, the question of whether there is a duty to die proves quickly moot. Such a duty would on Kantian terms both violate the concept that all human beings have "intrinsic worth" and have to be the result of a "self-defeating" imperative.

in which to engage in such debate. Instead I wish simply to meet the issue head on, not by responding to others but by offering an alternative approach to ethical questions concerning obligation and duty. In fact, the radically empirical account to be given does have affinities with the "correlation" model that rights theorists propose, but the correlation is not between "rights" and "obligations"; instead, the correlation is grounded in the universal human psychology of expressing desire through "claims."

In order to develop this account of "duty" and "obligation," it is worth beginning from the observation that "ethics" has multiple meanings. First, many of us carry with us the colloquial meaning that "ethics" is concerned with how each individual deals with "right" and "wrong," "good" and "bad." We talk about our personal ethics, and frankly most, if not all, of us believe we are good people who have "ethics." This sense of ethics is tied closely to *values* and *character*. Second, we recognize that as members of a profession, we might be governed by "ethics." This governing is often manifest in "codes," but it also resides in our sense of what being a professional is all about – for example, the responsibilities and obligations that come with the actions we perform in our roles as healthcare professionals. This sense of ethics is often associated with judgments of what are *right* and *wrong*. Third, we carry with us our values and interests, and we begin to recognize that others, too, have their own interests. Further, the roles we play, not only as professionals but as family members, friends, citizens, religious (or non-religious) believers, each carry corresponding obligations. Often, between personal interests, cultural values, professional and relational obligations, it is not uncommon to find ourselves in conflict with others, with institutions, even with the many aspects of ourselves. Here, conflicting concerns often lead to questions concerning ends we really should pursue and what means are appropriate in those pursuits. This sense of ethics can be characterized as weighing *good* and *bad*, *better* and *worse*.

No one of these three senses can be ignored, nor is it clear that these are reducible.[3] It is worth noting that each of us is a "values

---

[3] John Dewey has made this case in his essay "Three Independent Factors in Morals" (1930) and in his co-authored book, *Ethics* (1932, with James Tufts).

carrier," whether as a product of biology, nurturing, education, or some other means. Further, we do in fact find ourselves in relation to others – familial, professional, and so forth – and those relationships commit us to others and to expectations for which we are held accountable. Finally, in a finite universe of limited abilities and resources, with a plurality of individual and communal interests, we are confronted often by concerns for what we should do, and why. Ethics, then, concerns each of these aspects of moral living – values (character), duties (roles), and goods (ends).

In lieu of other ethical formulations of duty and obligation, William James offers his own take on the issue. In his famous essay "The Moral Philosopher and the Moral Life," James says, "[*T*]*here is some obligation wherever there is a claim.* . . . [E]very *de facto* claim creates in so far forth an obligation" (1891, 617). According to James, constitutive of a personal claim is a corresponding request that this claim be satisfied in the context in which it arises. James makes no appeal to "rights," nor is his sense of obligation equivalent to deontological duty. He is *not* here using the term "obligation" to denote the *outcome* of an adjudication of claims, nor as that which follows from a moral imperative. That is, he is not saying that simply because I request a car and you have one, you *must* give it to me. Instead, James's "claim" is descriptive of lived experience wherein individual activities (i.e., claims) place into the conversation of the community the need to recognize said claims.[4] As John Dewey explains, we do in fact deal with claims arising from our activities implicitly:

Some activity proceeds from a man; then it sets up reactions in the surroundings. Others approve, disapprove, protest, encourage, share and resist. Even letting a man alone is a definite response. Envy, admiration and imitation are complicities. Neutrality is non-existent. (1988 [1922], 16)

---

[4] There is debate in the secondary literature about what James means by "claim" here. On the one hand, James himself slips among the terms "claims," "ideals," and "demands." While I have chosen to see "claims" as descriptive of a certain kind of lived experience, experience that may be captured alternatively by "ideals" or "demands" depending on perspective, much more hangs on the interpretation of this term for the moral understanding of James by the likes of Roth (1969), Myers (1986), Gale (1999), and Cooper (2002), and I leave it to them to work through the confusion.

In a different voice, under a different guise Dewey and James are saying the same thing. People make claims, perform actions, and express desires, and others who have the resource to meet the claim are, in the broadest sense of the term, obligated. They are obliged to recognize, reconstruct, redirect, and respond to the claim in conjunction with their own activities. This is not "obligation" in the sense proposed by rights theorists, nor is it duty as the deontologist conceives it. This obligation is more basic and pre-critical, and recalling the language from the previous section, I shall call it a "*de facto*" obligation. In order to move from *de facto* obligations to "*ethical*" obligations, however, takes critical reflection upon our present and anticipated obligations to determine which obligations to fulfill and which to let drop. While *de facto* obligations arise with every expressed desire, a truly ethical obligation only results from the reflective process of weighing competing claims and their corresponding obligations – for example, an investigation of my desire to have a car versus your desire to keep your money or your car.

Ethics, then, begins with concrete claims that produce existent obligations, but the "moral philosopher" (which we all are) cannot rest there. Her task is to develop creatively an inclusive story that captures the vast array of interests at play. James's own injunction is "*Invent some manner* of realizing your own ideals which will also satisfy the alien demands" (James 1891, 623). James's radically empirical morality thus, insists that our acts of "invention" (meliorism) are necessary in order to fashion a solution that attempts to take *all* moral ideals seriously. That is, in order to arrive at an ethical outcome, we must adjudicate *existing claims*, intelligently and imaginatively devising a way to fulfill as many as possible. We must responsibly decide in light of all *de facto* obligations which to satisfy and which to let slide. The decisions will be troubling, and we will be called to account for them, as those whose demands go unsatisfied will rightly require of us an account of our decision making. So once again we are confronted with the demand for inquiry, which must be addressed, as we have said, by way of the radically empirical attitude, taking experience and meaning where we can find them, and employing narrative intelligence to the adjudication at hand.

Once more: What James is saying is that there are, *de facto*, obligations placed on us with the manifestation of each new claim. *Every* expressed claim places us in a position that demands that we recognize it and react to it. And it is our task to decide which to pursue and which must fall away, recognizing that the challenge of such a moral philosophy means that some ideals, in James's words, will be "butchered," and demands for their inclusion in future considerations will continue – our *de facto* considerations must be addressed anew.[5]

I wish to start with this Jamesian understanding of *de facto* "obligation," this basic kind of responsibility that arises from everyday desires expressed by ourselves and others. We cannot end there, of course, for we must press on to the end of moral inquiry in the realization of "ethical" obligation. Individual claims are real, but can be counter and conflicting. From this radical empiricist starting point, however, *de facto* obligations begin to bring to light a very interesting perspective.

Certainly in the Jamesian sense of the term, we have many obligations. Since we are caught up in social relationships, it would be virtually impossible not to have them. People constantly have desires and make claims that demand their time and energies. Furthermore, we might even extend the notion of a "claim" to "nature" itself – that is, to the environment at-large.[6] Natural resources become depleted

---

[5] I have not pointed out potential weaknesses in this Jamesian account. I take it as a reasonable account of ethics in light of taking on a radically empirical attitude. However, others may find reasons to reject this as a reasonable account of ethics, regardless. See, for example, the critique of James's moral philosophy in the recent book by Robert Talisse and Scott Aikin, *Pragmatism: A Guide for the Perplexed* (2008). There is a strong argument that is motivated primarily by the fact that James's position does not recognize that some "demands ... [simply] would be *immoral* to meet" (115). I am not persuaded, however, that they have made the case for the kind of moral "intuitionism" – what they call "common sense moral commitments" (116) that grounds their critique. James's claim, which I agree with, is that no such "common sense" claims can be made *a priori*. Only experience and reflection can determine which demands must go unsatisfied. I do think it is safe to say, though, that some demands will, by the very nature of the "costs" involved in satisfying them, have a much harder time being justified, and thus they will *practically* never move from *de facto* to *de jure*.

[6] James himself would most likely not extend the concept of *de facto* obligation to include claims by the environment. More precisely, the environment for James

and species near extinction, and these issues call out for our intervention. Given all this, we could scarcely avoid having *de facto* obligations of one form or another even at the ends of our lives. However, this does not tell us whether there are any particular obligations in the dying process. That is, simply because we are confronted with a wide variety of claims that demand our attention, this alone does not determine what the resulting obligations actually will be. *That* they are is true enough. *What* they are is still in question.

"Living" Obligations

Within a six-month period, 86-year-old Mrs. W. suffered one injury after another, each leading to greater, chronic debilitation:

Sustaining a hip fracture from slipping in her home led to hospitalization. The resulting post-operative care led to a nursing home. Soon thereafter she suffered respiratory arrest, leading to ventilator dependence and putting her back into the ICU of the local medical center. Within a few months, she suffered cardiac arrest, leading to severe anoxic encephalopathy. Mrs. W. then rests for almost a year in an acute care medical facility, diagnosed in a persistent vegetative state.

Mrs. W's husband of more than fifty years was distraught, pleading for continued therapy – a request that is troubling to the ICU staff. Meanwhile as Mrs. W. lay in the hospital, her bills continue to mount, covered by Medicare and private insurance, to the tune of three-quarters of a million dollars.

Mrs. W's situation is tragic, indeed.[7] Given her prognosis and her age, the responsibilities for and cost of care are enormous. While Chapter 5 will have more to say on the ethics surrounding medical conditions where patients are chronically incapacitated, Mrs. W's is but one of a number of cases, with different injuries and illnesses, that raise concerns about whether or not patients should remain under medical care, encumbering family, caregivers, and other resources.

cannot make claims. However, in light of a great deal of environmental theory and my own prejudices, I will assert the possibility of a claim-making environment in order to make the point that *de facto* obligations are with us in virtually every aspect of our lives.

7 In fact, this is the well-publicized case of Helga Wanglie (see, among many other accounts, Cranford 1991).

Or are there significant moral reasons for at least some such patients to find themselves obligated to die in order to ameliorate the burdens their care places on others?

In 1997, following on the heels of comments by then-governor Richard Lamm of Colorado, philosopher John Hardwig, in what proved to be a provocative and controversial article in the *Hasting Center Report*, took up directly the question "Is there a duty to die?" Hardwig's answer – that such a duty can certainly be operative in some patient's lives. In particular, he argues that as a result of the new technological circumstances that exist in most modern medicine, the fact that we are intimately related to others and our actions affect them deeply, and because of the concern of burdening our loved ones, the duty to die is real in very specific contexts for some people whose dying is burdensome and only after a rich, full life. His is not a justification of policy, but instead an argument for individualized, contextual decision making about the morality of dying (Hardwig 1997b).

In many aspects of his account, Hardwig and I agree that a kind of operative duty can arise. As Howard Brody has commented, "Hardwig...locat[es] the question of a duty to die firmly within an individual's narrative of value and narrative of relationships. Only the person herself and members of a close circle of intimates would be in any position to judge whether such a duty exists" (2003, 256). However, it is important to note that in arguing for his position, Hardwig specifically eschews any attempt to "theoretically" ground this duty. The foregoing account in this chapter gives a radically empirical basis for moral duties and obligations. Given the analysis, I, unlike Hardwig, do not eschew theory in order to ground the following attempt to address whether a specific "duty" to die exists based on this radically empirical philosophy.[8]

---

[8] To be clear, Hardwig and I agree on a great many points, though his "non-theoretical" approach seems unable to ground effectively his emphasis on a "burden to others" as the primary measure of when a "duty to die" might arise. Also, though he and I agree that the contexts of specific cases is necessary to determine the existence of a duty to die, we differ in that Hardwig believes that the existence of this duty for particular individuals is much more widespread then I believe it to be. I assert that without a concrete claim, no obligation exists. Burden, though often

While this concept of "obligation" can be applied to the lived experiences of individuals in the full bloom of health, it also applies equally to the experiences of dying persons. What then would be necessary for the existence of an obligation to die? Recalling James, this question is easily answered: The obligation to die can only arise from some concrete claim whose fulfillment entails someone's death. That is, in order for such an obligation to exist, someone must have a desire that in its consequences eventuates in a person's death. For example, insurance companies cut off payments; hospitals need bed space; healthcare staffs are stretched to the limit; families suffer emotionally and financially. Each one of these situations can call forth a very real, albeit sometimes cautious, desire for the patient to pass on. Of course, desires that someone die that are set forth by "heartless" insurance companies or "greedy, selfish" relatives may be easily dismissed, but note that even these desires are already post-critical, and not simply *de facto*, in that they are already negatively determined to be "heartless" and/or "greedy."

For those in the throws of a terminal illness or injury, obligations arising from the claims of loved ones, professionals, and even institutions are acutely felt. Dying persons often clearly recognize the pressures that bear on them concerning their continued existence – pressures from family, HMOs, nurses, economics, and so forth. Also, it cannot be under-recognized that *dying persons, themselves, may wish to die is a controlled way that, as they see it, retains dignity.* And still others who are (for whatever reason) incapacitated to the point of not being able to process such demands (the neurologically demented, permanently vegetative state patients, and so on) may, nonetheless, be the focus of even stronger claims on their lives (or, should I say, deaths).

difficult to bear, does not itself constitute a claim to end a life; thus, burdens that do not lead those who are burdened to make claims that entail someone's death cannot, on my account, ground an ethical duty to die. Finally, Hardwig's article is much more ambitious than my own discussion herein, and therefore attempts what mine does not – namely, support strongly the duty to die. My more modest argument is that it is entirely possible, even probable, that there are particular individuals whose universe of concrete claims and *de facto* obligations does entail, upon reflection, an ethical obligation to die. See other comments and critiques of Hardwig's position in Hardwig 2000.

It thus seems quite clear that many individuals have at least *de facto* obligations that implicate the desire for them to die. However, this fact alone does not settle the *moral* issue; in fact, it actually helps to highlight the need for moral deliberation, because while many individuals may be pressed by the force of *de facto* claims that, in turn, call for an obligation to die, it is not yet clear whether in the fullest ethical sense of the term, these individuals "ought"[9] to die. This fuller sense *begins* with Jamesian-type obligations *but does not fully take hold* until it is shown to be the end of a complete, reflective inquiry into all standing and anticipated obligations carried by the individuals who are affected by these obligations.

The task is therefore to evaluate any *de facto* obligations to die in light of other existing obligations. Claims on bed space, for money, or by insurance carriers compete with the desires of loved ones, not to mention the historical obligations of physicians to "do no harm." Personal interests in being with loved ones conflict with desires to cease the suffering or "pointless" existence. Deep cultural biases arise even as individual desires are expressed. As Hilde and James Lindemann Nelson point out, "the stakes are high, and yet, [i]t will sometimes turn out that the moral thing for a family member [or even close friend or physician, I have argued] to do is to kill or assist in the suicide of a dying loved one" (1995, 153). That is, *to the extent that no over-riding desires or obligations trump an existing obligation to die within the context in which it arises,* someone might find herself "ethically" obligated to die, in the deepest sense of that term. That is, we may find very real cases where patients upon thorough reflection are better off taking a path that leads to a quick, immanent death than one that lets them "hang on." On the other hand, if other conflicting obligations prove to be more important, more worthy of pursuit – that is, more valuable – no ethical "duty" to die will exist.

Now, unlike Kantian moral theory, the pragmatic sense of obligations does not presuppose a categorical duty to which desires and

---

[9] It is important to note that a moral "ought" is *not* equivalent to an "eternally enforced duty."

actions must conform in order to be considered ethical. As Mead puts it, "The moral question is not one of setting up a right value over and against a wrong value; it is a question of finding the possibility of acting so as to take into account as far as possible all the values involved" (Mead 1938, 465). Nor does it contain any prohibitive restrictions on "acceptable" or "unacceptable" obligations *a priori*. Thus, an obligation to die is a very real *possibility* (though its *probability* may still be dubious). And the decision as to whether a particular obligation to die is an ethical obligation will be based primarily on consequences and not intentions. However, contra the utilitarians, these consequences need not conform to a pre-defined aspirational "good" narrowly defined, where it becomes simply a matter of "greatest good for the greatest number." In fact, pragmatically, "the happiness of all is [not] worth more than the happiness of the individual but [instead], being what we are, we have to continue being social beings, and society is essential to the individual just as the individual is essential to society" (Mead 1938, 460). In other words, utilitarian notions need a great deal of reconstruction and naturalization if they are to function pragmatically. The social and environmental contexts that interact with individuals, and out of which any specifically felt obligation to die arises, will help dictate the uniquely defined good that only comes into existence as the outcome of our reflective activities.

"Duty" to Die?

In the end, the radically empirical answer to the question of whether or not there exists a duty to die requires a highly qualified answer – like Hardwig's, it must be contextual, but is further grounded in a particular take on what constitutes moral obligation. So we can say that there may be many different kinds of *de facto* obligations to die, and it is possible that *some* of these may be reconstructed into a variety of ethical obligations to die. That is, each obligation is itself unique to the situation in which it arises, and the inquiry that transforms that "mere" obligation into an ethical "duty" will itself create a uniquely felt duty to die.

However, it is important that my point not be misunderstood. The preceding argument does not entail the necessity of an "ethical" obligation or "duty" to die. In fact, there may be contervailing demands that entail for some a moral duty to *live*, even in the face of great suffering. However, the central point is that the argument does entail that *there be no necessary, a priori prohibition against a duty to die*. Given the virtually infinite number of situations in which dying persons find themselves, it is quite possible that many are obligated to die in the Jamesian, or *de facto*, sense, and some, though fewer, of them find themselves obligated in the fuller, "ethical" sense.

In other words, my argument here is that we do not rule out the very real, yet heartbreaking, possibility that some people in their unique situations in this world may have an ethical obligation to die. For anyone to pronounce *a priori* that a duty to die does or does not exist is foolhardy at best and bad ethics at worst. We limit the possibilities within the human condition whenever we make such pronouncements. This is not to say that such an ethical obligation would not be tragic, but in our limited, finite existence with our limited, finite powers, tragedy is all too much a part of our lives, and it cannot be eradicated by ethics. *Every* decision that leads us down one path permanently bars others; they are forever lost to us. This is tragic indeed. By analogy, every death wrenches from the community a unique participant, leaving a hole in her place, but this reality does not forecolse the very real possibility that some individuals may find themselves obligated to die in the very deepest, ethical sense of that term.

Must We Live and Die with the Tragic?

Having discovered the possibility of the existence of an albeit tragic obligation to die, what then are we to do? If such an obligation does exist, does it follow that others, *ipso facto*, have the right to enforce the obligation on a patient? The answer is clearly "no." Even if, say in the case of Mrs. W., that her condition warrants an ethical obligation for her to die, nothing is settled as to how that should occur, for the obligation does not, in itself, warrant family, friends, or healthcare professionals to kill her. In fact, her family is against such an action, and their rights as decision makers for her would necessarily need to be considered in the situation.

So, should we legislate activities in light of this new ethical insight? Can we bring societal pressure to bear on persons in the throws of such an obligation? What are our possible avenues of conduct? It does seem clear that we should tread lightly here; the "tragic" nature of the obligation highlights this fact. Unlike any other obligation, the fulfillment of an obligation to die is a final act for and of the person who does die. That is, it results in the death of a human being, and as such we should always keep a cautious eye out for the possibility of abuse – a rush to judgment, prejudice generalizations, and so on. Also, "blanket" responses to such obligations are not only fraught with danger, they run counter to the particularity of the obligations themselves. Thus, simply to discover that a specific ethical obligation to die exists in a given situation *does not entail* the need to create social policy to enforce said obligation. That is, we should not *legislate* that these ethically obligated people be killed, either through their own means or at the hands of another. Though we may wish to act in such a way that implies that one "ought" to die, legislating activities to bring about the fulfillment of such obligations may not be in our best interests as a society. And it is not unusual to make this kind of distinction between ethical obligation and legally demanded enforcement. Clearly there are many cases where economically well-to-do people have ethical obligations to distribute their wealth to those who are not as well off. Some people simply have more than they could ever use, and others obviously do not have nearly enough. After an inquiry into the many cases that exist of this kind of economic imbalance, it is quite plausible that some of the "rich" should give to the "poor." However, we do not legally enforce that obligation, favoring instead at the social policy level, to protect individual wealth and property. And yet this does not preclude grassroots organizing to bring pressure to bear where ethical obligations are not fulfilled. Now, to a much higher degree, an ethical obligation to die, like the obligation to distribute wealth, burdens particular individuals who are obligated in unique and vital ways. And it is the extreme nature of an obligation to die that, I would argue, precludes the use of not only legislative but general social pressures in order to "force the hand" of the one who is to die.[10]

Death, though it can affect many others, is only the end for a particular individual. The arguments in this book do not advocate a singular approach to all end-of-life situations. In fact, it is clear that so many complex factors exist in each patient situation that we will morally fail if we do attempt to apply one approach to all. Thus, in light of some specific obligation to die, the conduct toward that end should account for the sensitive nature of the particular situation. Rather than legislation or institutional demand, personal counseling, friendly advice, and family support can all help to make the burden easier to bear. Of course, at least two things should be noted. (1) There is a fine and often difficult to define line between counseling and coercion. Family and friends who look to gain personally have conflicts of interest that may negatively affect both the process of reflection on *de facto* obligations and the actions of persons who do find themselves ethically obligated to die. But even in less intentional ways, physicians, nurses, families, and friends can unwittingly but problematically take hold of the conversations about the dying patient, imposing interpretations and evaluations that are not well justified or reflective.[11] In no way am I advocating such coercive, conflicting behaviors, and I am advocating careful reflection and sincere discourse. (2) It may be the case that truly ethically obligated individuals refuse to satisfy or avoid fulfillment of their obligation to die.

---

[10] Some take a "duty to die" to entail "rights-language" (Cohn & Lynn in Hardwig 2000, 151), and specifically "a right to kill" (Callahan 2000, 141). As should be clear by its philosophical derivation in this chapter, and as I shall argue further in the next chapter, no such entailment need follow (cf. Hardwig 2000, 165), nor does it follow from the decidedly Jamesian account I have given. "Claims" or "demands" are not themselves "rights," and "obligations" (even "moral" ones) entail responsibilities on those who carry them. They may or may not invite others to participate; they may or may not require others to participate. That is, the connection back from duty to right is not a necessary one for the radical empiricist.

[11] In her excellent book . . . *And a Time to Die* (2005), medical anthropologist Sharon Kaufman explores the complex relationships among medical institutions, healthcare professionals, patients, and families at the end of life. Her account shows clearly the need for careful and sensitive reflection on how individual care is influenced by meanings that come from these complex relationships and the cultures of which they are a part.

And in the face of something so extreme and final, it should be no surprise that some are unable to muster the moral courage necessary to end their lives. In these cases, like so many others, we who look on are entitled to our moral disappointment or even outrage, but it seems wrong in a society that values individuality and individual expression to turn such disapproval into force or coercion.

Finally, if we do not like the possibility that concrete ethical obligations to die might exist for some people and therefore ought to be fulfilled, then clearly our only recourse is to act in such a way as to make the claims that create such obligations disappear. Analogous to the pragmatic idea that no ethical obligation exists *a priori* is the equally pragmatic idea that obligations can be diffused if the circumstances in which said obligations arise change. Thus we can remove an obligation to die by reconstructing the situation that helped cause its corresponding claim to be expressed. In other words, we should eliminate as far as possible the pressures experienced by patients that arise in difficult, chronic cases. We must attempt to abolish economic factors that plague medical treatment options, particularly for chronic-care patients. We should redesign the insurance industry to help support the necessary economic changes. We must develop better medical practices for the alleviation of suffering and the promotion of good dying processes in conjunction with health-care institutions. We can work with patients and their families to offer a support structure that makes their participation more important and vital to patient care. In sum, we must work to strengthen life-sustaining experiences within a life-sustaining environment. We must *enact* our hopes that no one is ever faced with such an obligation. We must also realize, however, that the day may come when such an obligation to die, tragic as it is, may arise and "ought" to be fulfilled. We can and should mourn the loss, and work toward a future where it *never* "has to" happen again.

Time to Refocus

Now, at the end of three chapters, we have developed an account of radically empirical morality that demands that all experience be considered in our philosophy and in turn requires a sensitivity at the level of particular interests and obligations. From this we have shown that morality may require that tragic obligations be fulfilled primarily by (or through, if you wish) patients.

What has not been articulated as clearly (though the implications are present already) are the roles that family, friends, and especially healthcare providers should play in ethically acceptable dying processes. The remaining chapters will attempt, though not exclusively, to speak to just those moral implications and requirements for those in relation to and in community with several different populations of dying patients.

4

Needing Assistance to Die Well

PAS and Beyond

> People die the way they live. I heard this many times from those
> who struggled for a simple answer to my prying questions.... "If you
> understood my life," they'd say, "you'd understand my death."
>
> *Lonny Shavelson*

> To understand with one's heart the pain of others is an attribute of
> the Divine.
>
> *Ronald Valdiserri*

In Chapter 3, I argued that there are conditions under which some
few persons may find that their dying experiences place tragic obligations on them. While the locus of moral concern in that chapter revolved around the patient (as it does in every chapter), there
has been important acknowledgement throughout that a radically
empirical take on values and meaning implicates others as well. This
chapter extends the moral implications of our account of significance and obligation for end-of-life care. This "extension" comes by
way of a focus on experience within a context familiar in medicine,
and yet resides at the margins of individuality and society – situations
that involve the issues of euthanasia and assisted suicide. In particular, I wish to explore two aspects of the dying process and our

Much of this chapter is adapted from Hester 1998.

attitudes toward meaningful acts of dying through suicide, assisted suicide, and euthanasia: (1) why and how some of us might wish to die differently, and (2) why and how those of us involved with dying persons might help in their dying processes.

Quite simply, though controversially, since many people who are left to the ravages of disease and bodily decline die horrible, painful, lonely, "undignified" deaths, it is understandable that some of these individuals would wish to have some control over these final acts of living. Further, significant and meaningful acts of living, consisting of the fusion of personal ideals and the fortitude to attempt carrying them out, are no less possible for dying persons than for those in the full bloom of health. Uniquely meaningful creative acts can occur even here at the end of life, where dying patients wish to "write" their narratives according to their own desires. These acts occur in a complex web of relationships that affect and implicate many people, and in the dying process, family, friends, lawyers, insurance companies, and medical professionals all play important roles, accounting for and participating in the life of the dying person. On those occasions when thoughtful, reflective individuals make decisions to end their lives on their own terms through suicide, assisted suicide, or euthanasia, those who are involved with these patients run the risk of true moral error if they simply ignore or deny these patients' wishes. They condemn dying patients to die alone through meaningless biological processes and indifferent acts of medicine. Instead, I suggest that we often have within our powers the ability to help these people end their lives in the bosom of a loving community through significant activities of their own making, and under certain circumstances this is the morally right thing to do.

Why and How We Might Wish to Die on Our Own Terms

Death is the end of living, but as we have already noted, dying is a process within living. As such it should not be surprising to ask if we might be able to die "better." As discussed in Chapter 1, death most often is not pretty; it is uncontrolled and unwanted. It seems reasonable that should we find ourselves in situations where death is foreseeable given current medical conditions (like the stories of Mr. S.

or Ramon from Chapter 1), we might desire to have a hand in our deaths to the extent that we shape our deaths to our liking and to the liking of those around us (cf. Davidoff 2002). If we truly are narrative selves, then dying is part of that narrative, a part that we might wish to shape creatively like so many other events in our lives. Following the discussion of Chapter 3, I wish to call attempts at shaping the dying process "meaningful" insofar as they mirror the shape of other acts of living that we consider significant and meaningful, and I want to suggest that a meaningful death is neither insensible nor impossible.

Why Someone Might Wish to Die

Jim Wichter is a veterinarian and horse farmer. A high school football player, a collegiate wrestler, a large man with once-strong legs and powerful hands, his wife now must lift him from his bed into a wheelchair. Jim has ALS, gradually losing muscle control from the legs up.

His wife, Suzie, pushes him, bathes him, shaves him, worries for him, loves him. At the same time, she admits frustration, exhaustion, and depression. Her sacrifices, their sacrifices, extend to all aspects of their lives. The family finances and estate have been reduced by half, and the time and energy to care for the caretaker is non-existent.

Jim realizes that medical technology – ventilators, feeding tubes, and medications – might keep him alive for years, but as his symptoms progress and loss of function continues, Jim sees a time when, like he once did for his suffering animals, he would want to die peacefully with assistance, not prolonging his time bedridden and completely physically dependent. As he begins to breakdown, he exclaims, "It is a terrible ordeal for me, . . . and it's even a more terrible ordeal for my family. And I just need it – I just need to go ahead and finish it."[1]

With our well-developed understanding of situated, progressive "meaning," we can begin to see that potential significance through the development of ideals and their achievement (whether "grandiose" and long-term or everyday and more immediate) can arise out of any of life's situations. Furthermore, Larry Churchill has argued for the moral primacy of life stories over other ways of

---

[1] Adapted from the story of Jim Wichter from the 2000 PBS series *On Our Own Terms: Moyers on Dying*, "A Death of One's Own."

understanding the processes of dying, calling for a thick sense of narrative, stating, "The narration of the meaning of death [read: "dying"] does not follow...a chain-like sequence, but follows a story line..." (Churchill 1979).[2] Dying thus has narrative significance for those whose experiences are touched by it.

In other words, opportunities for significance are "with us really under every disguise" (James [1899b], 653). As a matter of fact, we might find that "vital significance...blossoms sometimes from out of the very grave wherein we imagine that our happiness was buried" (James [1899a], 640). Even in the depths of despair, ideas can come to us; our "sick-rooms have their special revelations" (James [1899a], 645). Echoing this insight when speaking of the courage of some chronically and terminally ill patients, psychiatrist Arthur Kleinman states, "It [is] precisely situations of utter despair and terminality that [are] essential to create authentic meaning" (Kleinman 1988, 142). He continues later, "Meaning is created out of the context of serious illness....The meaning of illness need not be self-defeating; it can be – even if it often isn't – an occasion for growth, a point of departure for something deeper and finer" (Kleinman 1988, 144). In other words, in the face of the abyss of death itself, we might just find some last meaningful, progressive ["growth" enhancing] moments.

But here we may find ourselves taken aback by a collection of terms that seem paradoxical: 'terminal,' 'ill,' 'death,' 'abyss,' and 'progress.' If death is the final event of life (the end of possible futures) and the meaning of one's life is found in progress (which implies a future), how can we possibly relate death and progress? To handle this confusion, we need to come back to our focus on "dying" as a shift away from a focus on "death." This shift places emphasis on an active process, not on a singular moment or event. Emphasis on the process of dying highlights the potential for meaning at the end of life.

---

[2] William Gavin has a wonderful survey of philosophical approaches to death and dying (Kübler-Ross, Jonas, Veatch, Ramsey, Churchill, James, to name a few) in his book *Cuttin' the Body Loose* (1995) and the briefer book chapter On "Tame" and "Untamed" Death: A Jamesian Reflection (2003).

As a process, dying has its movement (as non-linear and chaotic as it might sometimes be) not only toward a final end – death – but it can have a movement toward a goal – dying well, a movement that can be directed by us through our determined activities and technologies. Given the nature of the process, this can be our final opportunity for meaning in life, and control over shape of the very character of the end itself. John J. McDermott expresses just this when he states that decisions about how one wishes to die are expressions of "refusal to have one's death announced by others, as though we were innocent bystanders to our own demise . . . [becoming] a true act of human freedom" (1986, 161).

Further, we must recognize that these processes go on in the world of living social beings; not only we but others become implicated in our activities and changed by them. Therefore, when death comes to our bodies, a part of us continues to the extent that others participated in the meanings of our lives and carry those meanings forth in their own lives after our bodies are gone.[3]

Dying with meaning, then, is transformative. On the one hand, it reshapes the lives of those who are left behind. It gives to their lives new grounds for future pursuits in regards to their own lives and dyings by engaging them in the meaning of dying for us. On the other hand, and maybe more importantly for the patient herself, dying with meaning empowers the patient in her final stages of living. It makes the patient a participant in the activities that surround the dying process. It explicitly treats the self as connected to meaning

---

[3] As a dying teacher once wrote to his student, "I am dying, and I know that you are afraid to die. So I am doing this for you. If I can do it, so can you!" (quoted in McDermott 2006, 271). Oliver Sacks also illustrates this sentiment well in speaking of his post-encephalitic patients at the closing of the "Foreword" to his book *Awakenings*: "[T]hose who have died are in some sense not dead – their unclosed charts, their letters, still face me as I write. They still live, for me, in some very personal way. They were not only patients but teachers and friends, and the years I spent with them were the most significant of my life. I want something of their lives, their presence, to be preserved and live for others, as examples of human predicament and survival" (Sacks 1990, xxxviii–xxxix). This sentiment is often portrayed by those dying patients who explicitly take on the role of being an example for others so that their death is not "in vain" but instead becomes meaningful to themselves and others (cf. Kleinman 1988, ch. 8 as well as Plato's *Apology, Crito* & *Phaedo*).

in life, as giving her some modicum of *authority* over her personal narrative. Meaningful acts of dying take the seemingly formless void of the abyss of death and give it a significant purpose while making it a meaningful achievement in the last stages of life itself; it turns potential nothingness into actual significance.

How Someone Might Wish to Die

"I think the hardest thing for me was to tell people that the time was short."

She walks with the help of a cane, awaiting visits from doctors and daughters alike. At 56, Kitty Rayl has lived the last 18 months with uterine cancer and its treatments, both aggressive and palliative, and what fight she could muster has now slowly become more and more in vain. After a life working, a total hysterectomy, several rounds of chemotherapy, loss of weight and strength, she now stays at home, requiring nurses and pills, people and prescriptions to provide her with some good days, while other days simply are a challenge to tolerate.

Kitty had long demonstrated an independent spirit where control of her life and circumstances were often paramount. She was a purchasing agent. Her concerns and fears are easily expressed. "I want to be able to read and be aware. . . . I don't want to be out of control. . . . I've always been one who wants control over things" she states. "I want everyday I can get . . . [but] I just can't think of anything worse than being helpless."

Kitty lives in Portland, Oregon and, exercising state law, has engaged Dr. C to help her die when she comes to the point that she has no dignity left.[4]

How does this definition of life's significance – progress – take shape for patients who are in the process of dying? For some patients, a significant dying process may involve specifically controlled means of securing death through suicide, assisted suicide, or euthanasia. These acts of acquiring death, at their own hands or at the hands of another deputized by them to do so, can empower patients and help to make their lives significant up to the moment of biological death. For many of the patients who consider euthanasia, the alternative to a chosen/controlled death is meaningless existence both created by and culminating in depression, suffering, and death.

---

[4] Adapted from the story of Kitty Rayl from the 2000 PBS series *On Our Own Terms: Moyers on Dying*, "A Death of One's Own."

In medical situations, it therefore becomes important to discuss the kinds of patients who find themselves dealing with (or involved in) end-of-life issues. Three groups of patients are of special concern here – the lucid yet terminally ill (discussed here), those who are permanently incapacitated (addressed in the next chapter), and children (specifically neonates) who are dying (covered in Chapter 6).[5]

The issues of control, participation, agency, and empowerment are central to a medical encounter. A patient with an illness already lacks a certain power and control in her life. In the case of a terminally ill patient, however, the issue of control is magnified by the gravity of the situation. To be characterized as terminally ill is to have a condition that is considered deadly and outside the reach of medicine's typical aggressive character toward curing.

A terminally ill patient with decision-making ability can be keenly aware of the abyss of death, which is marked by a complete lack of control; a terminally ill condition is itself a condition of diminishing control and a loss of self. While staring into this void, the patient often is fighting to retain health, control, and dignity – that is, to retain positive aspects of her very *self*. This abyss rarely is immediately desired, but the alternative – continued living – may hold a complete lack of significance or meaning heightened by pain and suffering and the inevitability of the nearing end. As our earlier discussions of meaning and dying show, however, dying can be a positively transformative process that changes the abyss of death into an idealized end to be controlled, manipulated, and achieved on terms that the terminally ill patient develops for herself. The character of the activities of the terminally ill patient who chooses suicide, assisted suicide, or euthanasia takes on a purpose and direction when she knows when and how death will come. Therefore some terminally ill patients take the opportunity to shape the end of their lives

---

[5] I will not be addressing the important and complex issues of chronically ill or injured patients such as those with long-term renal problems, extensive burns, or other debilitating problems that are difficult (if not impossible) to live with in a way meaningful to the afflicted individual but that are not, in themselves, fatal. There are possibilities for extending my argument to some such cases, but I will not attempt that here.

by creating a meaningful death, one that embodies an ideal to be realized through chosen, directed effort. For some patients, acts of suicide, assisted suicide, or euthanasia make the process of dying a vital part of their life stories; these acts constitute a controlled choice and activity that helps complete life on their own terms.

Cultivating a character that adjusts desired ends to the means available, and at the same time summoning up the fortitude necessary to fulfill goals in a life nearing its own end, opens up the possibility for a vast variety of satisfaction in the everyday things of life. Terminally ill patients who are capable of setting their sights on daily activities and personal contact while courageously accepting, yet looking beyond, their terminal condition give meaning to living in the process of dying. However, when most means and abilities are exhausted by disease or severe trauma and daily ends fade from view, very few possibilities for meaning are left. For patients in these conditions, then, the *choice* to die and the ability to control the dying process can become a last act of significance, a way to end their stories on personal terms. They might wish to be progressive *in* their dying, transforming the abyss of death by giving meaning to the end of their lives.[6]

For patients ravaged by a terminal illness, several options for controlling the dying process present themselves – suicide, assisted suicide, or euthanasia.[7] It is often the case, however, that the means of exercising the option of suicide are unavailable. This leads to the need for assisted suicide or euthanasia, where others help the patient by participating in these acts of dying.[8]

---

[6] There has been a good deal of research on the attitudes of terminally ill patients toward assisted suicide and euthanasia. Cf. Wilson, et al. 2007 and 2000, as well as Emanuel et al. 2000 and 1996, to name a few.

[7] While it may look here like a conspicuous omission, palliative and hospice care are discussed briefly at the end of this Chapter and in Chapter 6.

[8] Often there are good philosophical, logical, political, and moral reasons to divide issues raised by assisted suicide from those of euthanasia. This chapter focuses on lucid patients with decision-making capacity, for the balance of my argument, and to that extent I will put them both under the larger category of "assisted dying" at the patient's request. Later (see fn. 11, for example), I will note when conceptual clarity among these notions is important.

Why and How We Might Help the Dying

While there is an important sense in which death "establishes an unmistakable singularity," a recognizable "boundary [where] singularity is defined by death (in that death remains irreducible)" (Bliton and Finder 2002, 255), death almost never affects just one person – namely, just the one who dies. Death of a loved one affects others in a variety of ways. Certainly, there are those instances in which people who are dying have few if any ties to other individuals in society, but even their deaths affect government workers, hospital personnel, and so on. Small ripples from a small pebble, we might say, but any ripple affects the surrounding waters. At the other end of the spectrum, there are the deaths of well-connected individuals who made contributions not only to their own immediate circle of friends and family, but beyond. Some say, for example, that when JFK died, a part of the United States died with him. The deaths of prominent individuals act in this way as waves rather than ripples. More common, though, are the deaths of persons who have friends, and relate well enough with their families such that their deaths create a hole in the communal space they once occupied.

However, most tragic are those "connected" individuals who still die alone, particularly in those situations when dying individuals ask for help from family, friends, physicians, and so on in controlling their dying processes, only to be ignored and denied this last wish. A terminally ill individual reaches out for aid from a loved one or medical professional, requesting that this life be completed in a personally meaningful manner, and the other turns away, frightened by, confused concerning, or simply morally opposed to the plea. However, when others do not aid in a competent patient's intelligent request to die, they leave her alone at a time when remaining connected to others can be vital. More importantly, if life's significance comes from the development of ideals and the ability to achieve them, and if moral obligations can follow from the desires expressed by dying patients, when others turn away they condemn the patient desirous of a "noble" or at least "controlled" death to end her life in a state of complete lack of significance, and that is a moral failure to do justice to an integrated life with others. Thus they hold responsibility for taking away any ability for the patient to reach her final ideals.

If human dignity has any meaning, it comes from the personal participation in and intelligent development of one's life story by responsibly setting goals and meeting them through appropriate means at one's disposal. Meaningful living while dying can only come through recognizing and acting in such a way that we treat the dying as agents in life and participants in the community with love and support from the community. As discussed in Chapter 2, the self is an active member of society. We are situated beings meant neither to live nor die alone. *Those who would turn their backs on the cries of one who is dying do so at the expense of positively helping to shape the meaning of that person's final stages of life.*

Objections to Assistance in Dying

Of course, there are several objections to my stance that arise immediately. I will survey only a few of the more persistent ones here.[9]

The Unquestionable Good That Is Human Life

One objection states that the ending of life through our own human manipulations is wrong regardless of the dying person's desires. This is a position taken by some religious institutions such as the Roman Catholic Church and others (cf. Coleman GD 1987; Paris and Moreland 1998; Verhey 1998). This objection to euthanasia is based on the idea that human life is an unquestionable good that cannot be begged, borrowed, or stolen as its value transcends mere human existence on earth. This position is held by not just a few persons in our society but also by ethicists in the fray of end-of-life care debates. At one level, it is almost impossible to engage with this objection as it stems from a difference in ideology concerning human nature – that is, a metaphysical claim – that cannot be addressed in this work.

---

[9] A couple of possible objections that I will not cover can be found in articles both by R. Macklin and by E. Pellegrino in Beauchamp, ed. 1996 and Sulmasy 1995. Also, see the collection, *The Case against Assisted Suicide* (Foley and Hendin 2002) for arguments from various perspectives.

However, at another level, Lisa Bellantoni correctly points out that "the beliefs that centrally organize [the] moral lives" of "members of faith communities" are part of "their 'lived experience'" (Bellantoni 2003, 621). As such, a radically empirical attitude must account for these faith–communal beliefs. What can we say to this objection to aid in dying.

It may be a thin response, but the immediate retort seems clear: If the narrative selves engaged in these communities find that in belonging to these faith communities, their "eschatological visions under-write their lived experiences of health and illness" (Bellantoni 2003, 623), then their life stories should account for those values in determining morally appropriate ways of dying. That is, for most members of communities that hold to these transcendent values, no such concern for finding aid in dying will occur.

The danger here, though, is that at the same time it seems that these members' own values might in turn condemn them to die in horrible ways, cut off from the aid of caring measures that might hasten death. "Suffering," it would seem for some faith communities, is itself a good. Whether for a monastic ascetic of Christianity, Buddhism, or other religious conviction, there can be meaning in suffering, and my position would not deny that fact. However, "while the Christian tradition [for example] challenges the claim that all suffering is meaningless and needs to be ended, it urges compassion of those afflicted with undeserved and unexplainable sufferings," noting that "we are not obliged to hang on to physical existence" (Lewis 2000, 76). For some – Roman Catholics, for example – the rule of double-effect and the doctrinal division between "ordinary" and "extraordinary" care may be utilized to avoid the condemnation of unexplainable suffering at the end of life (though even these doctrines are in contention as of the early 2000s). Of course, neither of these moral instruments is uncontroversial, but the literature concerning these points and their detractors is vast, and I will leave that debate for others.

Instead, it would seem that short of either changing convictions about the transcendent good that is human life, or imposing such a value on all human beings regardless of their participation in faith communities that hold such beliefs, Bellantoni's objection is no objection at all. That is, so long as the belief is an individually held communal belief, the concern about aid in dying would seem not to arise. Since no further argument is put forth as to why individuals who are not part of the community should necessarily hold the same belief, Bellantoni's argument stands as a reasonable reminder that public policy should not require all dying persons to agree to some form of aid in dying from the medical establishment. To extend beyond Bellantoni's claim about individual faith commitments within a community to public policy would require a wider metaphysical claim about either the universal character of a particular human value, or an absolute claim about human nature that reaches beyond faith communities. Of course, no such policy argument is made or implied either by Bellantoni on behalf of faith commitments or by me on behalf of aid in dying. In fact, the argument throughout this book has been one from a pluralistic, radically empirical position – one that tolerates such claims *within* narratives but is suspect of claims when imposed "blindly" *across* narratives.

Technology as a Double-Edged Sword

A second objection to assistance in dying comes in the wake of great advances in medical technology. It is precisely the great leaps made in medical technology over the last forty years that today keep patients alive longer. If only we can keep a "dying" patient alive long enough, so the argument goes, some cure might come through. Technology is precisely the manifestation of human efforts to improve the existential situation of individuals. Medical technology is developed in specific response to the problematic situations that threaten our biological lives.

This position on technology, however, obscures the fact that the ever-changing and progressing field of modern, medical technology has a two-fold effect on ethics: (1) Yes, technology has allowed for increased abilities to affect a cure and to prolong and sustain the life of terminally ill patients; (2) but on the other hand, technology has dehumanized the medical environment by promoting technological solutions over human ones, sometimes at the expense of the patient's desire for meaning.

It is certainly the case that medical technology saves lives that even in the recent past would have otherwise been lost. Those who would promote technology's ability to cure illness and sustain life, however, must not be blinded by this ability. We must recognize the ridiculousness of vainly hoping for medical "magic bullets" in the face of late-stage fatal illness. This is not to say that particular patients who face what are now eventually fatal conditions, like Alzheimer's or Huntington's chorea, should give up on the future possibilities of medicine, but many others simply do not have that luxury. Though it would be foolish to believe that either euthanasia or assisted suicide is the best choice for every terminally ill patient (no matter how degenerated they are), it is equally foolish to believe that an eighty-year-old patient with metastasized cancer that has permeated multiple organs and glands should hold out for a cure.

Further, for those patients who do wish to die, the dehumanizing quality of technology is acutely felt. The lack of control over their life story that is created by the operations of medical instrumentation and machinery robs patients who are dying of significance. In sustaining life, then, medical professionals must always put the patient's interests first and make her the focus of the medical investigation and a participant in the treatment process. If a progressive, meaningful life is to be achieved, some forms of technology will be necessary, whether it be the use of forks and spoons or the employment of feeding tubes and intubation devices. Technology operates in this way as means to further goals of the patient. However, when technology is experienced as curbing the ability to live a significant life or die a meaningful death, we must move beyond technology.

Technology's ability to overpower human decisions is quite pronounced in medicine and must be held in check by keeping the focus of the medical encounter not so much on what medicine *can do* but on a patient's *fortitude and ideals* – that is, what constitutes significant living by and for the patient.

PAS, Politics, Professionalism, and Public Policy

A third objection to assistance in dying is one pointed primarily at forbidding the practice of physician-assisted suicide (a practice now well known in popular culture thanks to Dr. Jack Kevorkian), and while forms of this objection have come from at least three directions – politicians, medical professionals, and policy advocates – they focus on the belief that the profession of "doctoring" specifically excludes assisting in a patient's death.

In April 2002, The Netherlands became the first country to implement a law supporting medically performed euthanasia. Though this practice has gone untouched by Dutch courts for many years, the Dutch parliament finally enacted legislation creating legal protection and, more importantly, spelling out specific practice guidelines for medically performed euthanasia.[10] In September of that year, Belgium followed suit with its own euthanasia legislation.

Controversial as these laws are, both in Europe and out, the United States faced its own battle over aid in dying. On March 22, 2002, arguments were heard in Federal court in the case of *Oregon v. Ashcroft*, where nine plaintiffs (four of whom have since died) brought suit against the U.S. Attorney General John Ashcroft after his November 6, 2001 declaration that he had instructed the Drug Enforcement Agency to seize the license of any physician who prescribed lethal doses of drugs under Oregon's 1997 Death with Dignity Act. Using the Federal Controlled Substance Abuse Act as his justification, Ashcroft made his surprising announcement on Election Day. Within days, Federal Judge Robert Jones had issued a temporary restraining order against the U.S. Attorney General's order allowing the Oregon act to continue functioning until a judgment could be determined. That judgment went against Ashcroft (a judgment that was subsequently appealed to and upheld by the U.S. Supreme Court).

The Oregon law came into existence upon a vote of its citizenry in 1994. Almost immediately, suit was brought to stop it. By 1997 (and taking affect in 1998) the law was reinstated by another majority

---

[10] Recent research (reported on surveys given out in 2005) from The Netherlands on the percentage of deaths from euthanasia and on the reporting practices of physicians has been published by van der Heide et al. (2007). The data indicates that there has been a decline in the percentage of acts of euthanasia and PAS for dying patients since implementation of the law in 2002, and that there is an increase in the use of "terminal sedation."

(60 percent) of the voters in Oregon. The Oregon law, unlike the Dutch law, is an assisted-suicide law under which physicians can prescribe lethal doses of certain drugs but cannot actively give the medication to the patient. This leaves the patient as the final determiner of whether or not to die on these terms. As of 2009, several other states (including California, Hawaii, Maine, Vermont, and Wyoming) have considered, but rejected, legislation that would legalize assisted suicide; Washington state voters, on the other hand, endorsed an assisted suicide law similar to that of Oregon's in 2008.

For a functional definition, let us agree that physician-assisted suicide (or PAS) is any act in which a licensed physician aids in the death of a patient (a death desired by that patient) – the physician providing the medical means (typically prescribed drugs) but not herself inducing anything. The patient is the final and necessary actor. On the other hand, the term euthanasia, though variously defined throughout the ages and literature, will be used technically as an act by a medical professional where both the means necessary are provided and the final act is performed by said professional. (It may be helpful to note that PAS and euthanasia differ from foregoing life-sustaining treatments in that foregoing is readily accepted both ethically and legally as an extension of any patient's right to refuse treatment.)[11]

In the case of Oregon and Washington, therefore, patients are committing suicide that is directly aided by the medical establishment, while in The Netherlands, euthanized patients die not of their own hand but at the hands of another "deputized" (we might say) to do so. In the United States, the latter act is legally forbidden in every state, whereas the former has, as of 2008, been

---

[11] Wesley Smith in his book *Forced Exit* (1997) wrongly decides that terminology is unimportant here. In fact, he reduces both euthanasia and PAS to acts of "killing." The charged emotional, legal, and political character of "killing," makes this an unsuitable *reductio*. This is not to argue that the concept of "killing" is not applicable in some way, but there are significant practical differences that require conceptual clarity in order to make morally meaningful pronouncements about these clearly different practices. For a careful analysis of the distinction on moral and legal grounds, see Miller, Fins, and Snyder 2002.

accepted in two states, considered by others, and outlawed in most states.

It is nothing new to say that both euthanasia and PAS are controversial. Certainly many individuals have specific moral concerns with both types of activities, while institutions, professions, and states have chimed in as well. While no individual state needs a law to forbid assisted suicide (though it would need one to allow it – hence Oregon's and Washington's laws), many states have enacted a specific law prohibiting assisted suicide. Furthermore, professional organizations such as the powerful American Medical Association (AMA) have long decried so-called active euthanasia, and have also spoken out against PAS.

And yet when pronouncing on the very topic of PAS, the AMA states, "Physicians have an obligation to relieve pain and suffering and to promote the dignity of dying patients in their care." Unfortunately, this statement muddles their position: Whence do these two obligations arise, and are they always compatible? What is meant by "dignity," and how is it best promoted? Ironically, it is not unimportant to note that the term "dignity" is co-opted by the AMA from the "right to determine death" movement that has used (and, as we see, Oregon uses directly) the rhetoric of "dignity" to support its own claims to a painless death through PAS and other means. But since the AMA has come out against PAS, at least some of the constituents to the fray are equivocating on the term "dignity." While the Oregon law and its supporters claim that PAS promotes dignity, the AMA and others with their views do not accept a definition of 'dignity' that includes such practices as PAS and euthanasia.

Morally, however, when someone requests to die, an adjudication of that request involves reflection on how fulfilling this request might fit with other obligations already present. Particularly in the hospital setting, a patient's request to die usually falls on the ears of her physician. This seems only natural given that physicians are highly trained and have exclusive access to medicine and a privileged position of power within the hospital. But as implied by the AMA's policy, some physicians feel that moral conflicts arise over requests for euthanasia because it interferes with a physician's *prima facie* obligation to aid in healing. How are physicians to determine which obligation holds more weight? The struggle here is not merely a linguistic or definitional one over "dignity." It is not even just a conceptual one. It is clearly a practical matter, an ethical matter of the highest order because it forces us to confront what actions are right, good, and acceptable. It speaks not just to our values but to our character, and to the character not just of individuals but of institutions. This debate rightly has not gone on solely at the level of one-to-one interaction between physicians and patients but, as we have already seen, at the levels of the profession of medicine and of public policy.

Evidence of broadly professional concerns came in reaction to an infamous 1988 letter to the editor of JAMA describing the aided death of a patient known only as "Debbie." The anonymously written story drew quick, negative reaction from a group of well-known physician-ethicists – Willard Gaylin, Leon Kass, Edmund Pellegrino, and Mark Siegler. In their words:

This issue touches medicine at its very moral center; if this moral center collapses, if physicians become killers or are even licensed to kill, the profession – and, therewith, each physician – will never again be worthy of trust and respect as healer and comforter and protector of life in all its frailty. (Gaylin, et al. 1988, 2140)

Their argument, at its core, is based on the premise that constitutive of medicine is the *healing* relationship. As such, constitutive of the physician's practice of medicine is that the physician avoid activities that intentionally and actively end the life of a patient.[12]

It is important to see, however, that this statement is at best only *descriptive* of current medical practice. It says that the institution known as "physician" is defined in such a way as to delimit the practices of physicians, excluding active measures that "kill." What follows for physicians from this premise is that the trust, care, and compassion necessary to perform as healers pits any involvement in helping patients die ("killing" is their term) against the very nature of medicine itself. In other words, according to these physician-ethicists, there is no way both to perform adequately in the role of physician

---

[12] Others have made similar arguments as well. See, for example, Byock 1997, Baumrin 1998, and Kass 2002.

and to help patients die. This argument is psychologically powerful for its ability to speak to the character of the profession and institution of medicine itself. Of course, for it to be a successful argument and not just powerful, one must first accept both their characterization of medicine and what counts as caring, compassionate activity.

Even if we are to accept this seemingly constitutive rule for physicians, however, this does not exclude the possibility of aiding patients who desire to die. We could always create a separate institution sanctioned by society to practice euthanizing measures (or even simply expand the healthcare team that participates in such acts – cf. Faber-Langendoen and Karlawish 2002). The development of such a group of individuals (regulated in any number of ways) would free "physicians" of the task, thus allowing them to concentrate on curing and healing. In other words, the argument put forth by Gaylin, et al. does not preclude euthanizing measures that might be sanctioned by society.

Of course, we might also wish to respond to Gaylin et al. by problematizing their very notion of "physician" itself. Surely the very idea of being a physician has shifted throughout the centuries. From the earliest ancient texts, the role was deeply identified with a spiritual component. Subsequently it has evolved, and the spiritual character was deemphasized – for some, even eliminated. In the Middle Ages, being a physician meant the exclusion of surgical practices, and yet today surgery is a well-accepted specialty within medicine itself. Even the emphasis on careful and substantive scientific training and knowledge is relatively new, and controversy still remains in the guise of the struggle with the championing of evidence-based medicine to the detriment of experienced clinical judgment.

Specific to the charge at hand, however, a response on the role of physician as constitutively excluding PAS must focus on questioning the limited role of a physician in our society and the definition of "healer/comforter" as excluding acts of euthanasia. We certainly might wonder why humane means of death cannot be taken by a physician on behalf of a patient whose request is considered to be sincere and legitimate. My previous arguments should already make us suspicious – if not outraged – given that real moral obligations to some patients may not be satisfied in lieu of a suspect limitation on the nature of the medical profession. In fact, I have argued at length elsewhere (Hester 2001) that medicine should be concerned first and foremost with "living healthily," and that healthy living is to be found in connected, communal individuality – that is, an integrated, narrative self. Herein, I have argued that dying, as a part of living, must be taken up meaningfully in a narrative life. Thus, *meaning* in dying may require *aid* in dying by physicians dedicated to the healthy living of their patients.

And yet, beyond these narrower professional concerns, at the level of public policy, the debate has been joined on many fronts. One of the more famous and pervasive treatments and conclusions came in 1994 from the New York State Task Force on Life and Law. As recounted by bioethicist John Arras, the Task Force, though split among its twenty-five members on reasons for their conclusions, was nearly unanimous in its recommendation that PAS and active euthanasia not be supported by public policy and the law. Some simply took the absolute moral stance (both religiously and secularly argued) that such acts are unethical regardless of conditions or participants. Others believed (echoing Gaylin, et al.) that though someone may be morally justified in participating in such acts, physicians never are. Lastly, there were the "slippery slopists," who believed that though they would want someone to help them in their own time of need, and that there certainly could be morally justified acts of euthanasia, assisted suicide, and *physician* assisted suicide, the individual case could not be extrapolated into public policy without real danger that was too great to take on.

On empirical grounds alone, the slippery slope argument is, so far, not well supported (though every slippery slope position can always fall back on a wait-and-see attitude). For example, although in the eleven years (1998–2008) that Oregon's Death with Dignity legislation has been in effect the number of requested prescriptions and ingestions of lethal medication has risen, numbers remain notably low relative to the numbers of persons in Oregon who die each year (401 patients have died from suicide by legal, lethal medications since inception of the Act in 1998, with a ratio of 2:1000 (or 0.2 percent) PAS to other deaths in 2008 – see http://www.dhs. state.or.us/publichealth/chs/pas/pas.cfm).

It is interesting to note, however, that the need *for* a policy in support of PAS is betrayed in Arras's account (1997) of why the NY Task Force voted against PAS policy, for he himself notes that several members of the Task Force would appreciate having a Timothy Quill-like compassionate physician help them die should their own health deteriorate through terminal illness. However, once this is said, the argument against allowing such practices is undermined. That is, to claim it is morally acceptable to help some patients die and yet argue that it should be legally unacceptable is to say that one is willing legally to prosecute people who perform *morally good* acts. If this is the position, we allow prosecutors a good deal of discretion, which simply means that such decisions are subject to the political climate, individual values, and abuse of power. Certainly, such a position cannot be justified morally or practically (if these two can, in fact, be separated).[13]

Here, at the end of this discussion, suffice it to say that the cases of The Netherlands, as one (albeit still controversial) example, and Oregon, as another (less controversial), fly in the face of some very serious opposition. Add to this the federal government's crusade, and it can look as though wherever one comes down on the *ethics* of aid in dying, no *public policy* initiative has a chance.

Of course, this and the previous chapters have argued that it does matter where one comes down ethically on the subject, and much of the ethical grounding that argues against social acceptance for aid to the dying is flawed because it is not sufficiently sensitive to the radically empirical notion of narrative meaning in dying patients' lives. While I need only refer the reader to those previous discussions as supporting the possibility of developing carefully structured policy to allow for aid in dying in select and limited cases, this still may not satisfy some who have a more social view of how the "slippery slope" argument might take hold.

---

[13] For more about the importance of and concerns with PAS policies and guidelines, see Snyder, Caplan, and Faber-Langendoen (2002). Also Orentlicher and Snyder (2002) discuss the challenges of regulating PAS.

Revisiting the Slippery Slope

The slippery slope argument is not unique to the NY Task Force, and can be expressed in various ways. One well-developed argument comes from a fellow pragmatist, Mary Mahowald (2003), who applies the insights of Peirce's analytic framework, Addams's care ethic, and James's mediation to two possibly conflicting beliefs in order to see where the inquiry might lead. The beliefs are quite common to many of us: On the one hand, killing is wrong, and on the other, pain should be alleviated. Mahowald begins by using Peircean analysis of beliefs to express possible ideas of what it means to kill someone:

1. Killing means ending the life of someone.
2. Killing means letting someone die when one could prevent it.
3. Killing means helping someone to die.

This three-part distinction of possible meanings brings acts of murder, euthanasia, and assisted suicide all within the realm of killing, and Mahowald, as a "medical pacifist," wants to avoid every act that falls under any one of these three meanings. Thus, when pain relief through methods other than killing are ineffective, she is left in conflict. One resolution is to apply Addams's care ethics, which, Mahowald argues, is opposed to killing as well, but does allow the application of the rule of double effect (115).

To mediate fully the conflict, however, Mahowald takes seriously the idea that holding and acting on beliefs have consequences, both short and long term. As she points out, "the consequences [of assisted suicide] to be concerned about would necessarily stretch beyond those that affect particular patients, families, caregivers, to those affecting the larger society as well" (117). This squares precisely with our narrative account of the social self. For Mahowald, this insight leads to a serious consideration of how assisted suicide, if accepted socially, might affect society, and her concern is that such practices can lead from "negative eugenics" – foregoing life-sustaining measures – to "positive eugenics." Here the move seems to be that the "willingness to implement the desires of competent, dying, suffering persons" leads to "willingness to do this for those who are not dying, whose pain is relievable, and those who are incompetent.

Mere willingness in such circumstances could lead to something more onerous[–] . . . a readiness or desire to end the lives of those whose health status is severely compromised or costly to support" (118). In such an environment, pressures on specific individuals from "family members or social attitudes about the appropriateness of prolonging" become powerfully influential, and individuals within particular groups become vulnerable as targets of this pressure – for example, women and disabled persons[14] (119). Mahowald rightly notes that to develop morally sound social practices we must involve those who are affected by them – thus expanding the conversation and participation in a collaborative inquiry. And her conclusion is that "[t]o protect for all of us the right to die and to adequate pain relief, while ensuring that out right to life and dignity be respected no matter what our circumstances . . . demands the placement of wedges . . . along life's inevitably slippery slope" (120).

Mahowald's pragmatic argument and discussion are a challenge to those who favor allowing euthanasia and assisted suicide. Beginning from her stated beliefs and following her use of pragmatic insights and methods, it is clear that she takes seriously the call of radical empiricism to view all things in context, in the widest sense of experience. However, what strikes me is not only where she begins, but what she concludes.

Specifically, she begins with a very broad and general belief – killing is wrong – which she analyzes to include acts that would help others die, as well as acts that are more direct. This may be a reasonable analysis of the belief, and yet it is not clear that this belief is sufficiently nuanced to capture the belief-experience of many people. That is, it seems to be a slogan to say that killing is wrong, but is not necessarily a belief. Beliefs themselves are often more complex and practically robust, and in fact I would say that a careful investigation of my own beliefs would show I do not believe that all killing

---

[14] Of course, Mahowald is not the first or only person to be concerned about the affects of the acceptance of assisted suicide on the disabled population (cf. Gill 1992; Silvers 1998; Coleman 2002, among others), but I have chosen her argument since it comes from a pragmatic foundation that would seem to be a direct strike against my own use of pragmatism.

is wrong, but that *murder* is wrong or that *destructive violence against an innocent person* is wrong. Now, how these might be analyzed in a Peircean fashion I will not attempt here, but the point is that if one wants to hold to a general belief about the wrongness of "killing," it may indeed lead to the arguments that Mahowald puts forth about how to resolve the conflict between avoiding killing and alleviating pain. However, if one's beliefs do not already start at this general level, it is not clear that her argument is convincing.

Furthermore, even if her position on the belief-conflict applies broadly, the concern about the slippery slope, while coming out of a pragmatic account, is of a different sort. Specifically, it becomes a matter of empirical evidence, as well as of personal experience, to determine whether the concerns about the affects of implementing (P)AS or euthanasia practices when adults with decisional capacity request it are valid. Mahowald notes that, for example, "The [fact that the] great majority of patients whom Dr. Jack Kevorkian has helped to die are women suggests that women may be more likely than men to look for assistance because their sense of self-worth has been based primarily on their capacity to care rather than be cared for" (119). I am sympathetic to this reading of the situation, but as Mahowald also points out in her footnote to that sentence, it is possible the ratio is skewed simply because elderly women outnumber men. So, while her concern about disproportionate application of PAS to women (and, for that matter, other vulnerable populations) must be taken seriously, further analysis of the actual conditions and situations are necessary to draw the kinds of slippery slope concerns Mahowald points to.

Mahowald, however, is not alone in her concern. Advocates for the disabled and elderly (and other vulnerable persons – for example, Silvers 1998; Coleman D 2002; Cohn and Lynn 2002) also express unease about the slippery slope, in part because of both existing cultural prejudices, and the added social pressures that might be read into allowing assisted suicide and euthanasia. On the one hand, there is no denying that prejudice and marginalizing occur. Further, social practices, not just individual acts, affect individuals within a community. To this extent, there are legitimate concerns about how stigmatization already affects medical practices – from how physicians treat vulnerable populations to whether families always have the interest of their patient-family members at heart – and how social acceptance of PAS and euthanasia might supplement these prejudices. As Adrienne Asch has forcefully put it, "What needs to change is . . . the emotional and interpersonal environment; that environment can only change when professionals lead the way to supporting the capacities and thereby affirming the humanity of severely ill and imminently dying people" (2005, S34).

There are plenty of examples of healthcare professionals' inability to treat disabled and other vulnerable persons with the respect and compassion they do other patients, and yet having said this, there still remains the need for better empirical study, not just anecdotal examples. Issues have been raised about, say, the practices in Oregon since the implementation of the Death with Dignity Act (1997). Foley and Hendin (2002) note discrepancies and contradictions in the accounts of the first case of PAS under the Oregon law (also discussed by Coleman D 2002); they also note places where the law and the requirements for the Oregon Department of Health are unclear or unhelpful, and where information may be confusing, biased, or under-reported. All of this, it is argued by Hamilton (2002), is going on in a culture of silence and secrecy.

These reports and insights are disturbing, and may well speak to something deeply flawed or systemic, but they may not as well. Much of the discussion focuses not on the elements of the Oregon law but on individual cases, medical practices of some physicians, and the practices of groups such as Compassion in Dying or institutions such as Kaiser Permanente. And while it would not be surprising if we were to find that actions and procedures in a few of the over 401 cases of legal PAS in Oregon (as of 12/31/08) were questionable medically or morally, such questions alone do not constitute a systemic problem. More problematic are the claims that physicians poorly recognize clinical depression (cf. Ganzimi et al. 2008) or that institutions systematically develop black-box procedures to obscure their practices in this matter (Hamilton 2000). Again, though, save for an obvious need in education for physicians, neither of these speak to flaws in the law itself *unless* they speak to persistent and uncompromising cultural practices that make the law untenable to implement securely.

And yet is it then the case that no law could be well developed or that Oregon's law could not be adequately adjusted? No clear indication of witting or unwitting *targeting* of vulnerable populations has been demonstrated to date. And the issues that have been raised do not seem beyond repair, whether through education, procedural adjustment, or both. There is no doubt that public policy must be sensitive to injustices that the law might perpetuate, and yet it seems unwarranted to throw Oregon's law out without first attempting to adjust its procedures and requirements. Unless those who are concerned about vulnerable populations are also claiming that any sanctioned PAS is inherently flawed given their concerns (and that case has not been made, to my knowledge), there is room here for common ground.

Finally, the argument throughout this book has been that there is no *a priori* tenable argument to take PAS and euthanasia off the "ethical table." Further, the variability in individual patient stories is such that medicine applied as treatment of pain and suffering will not work for all patients. Some life stories (probably very few) are well ended with our aid. Mahowald is right to be sensitive to the environment in which any such practice is sanctioned, and there are certainly some environments that would undermine any positive moral claim for PAS and euthanizing practices. And yet I am not convinced that it has been demonstrated that public policy could not be developed (at least here in the United States) that can allow those few who need our aid to get it without fear of legal prosecution for either the dying patient or those who aid the dying. It seems that more work to "invent some manner" of satisfying these multiple concerns, claims, and desires needs to be done.

"Rights," "Obligations," and "Meaning": Should We Aid the Dying?
More prevalent an objection than the first two and more general than the third may be the following: To some it may be acceptable for reflective, terminally ill people both to desire and to take their own lives; however, moral prohibitions arise when others, any others, are asked to aid in carrying out this desire. This objection, in

conjunction with an objection to the idea of creating "meaning" through euthanasia, is illustrated, for example, by ethicist Daniel Callahan in his well-known essay "Self-Determination Run Amok."

Callahan begins with a central question concerning assisted suicide and euthanasia, "How are we to make the moral move from my right of self-determination to some doctor's [or other individual's] right to kill me – from *my* right to *his* right?" (Callahan 1992, 52) In a more recent essay, Callahan puts it this way: "Ought the general duty of the physician to relieve suffering encompass the right to assist a patient to take his or her own life if that is desired and seems necessary?" (Callahan 2002, 54) Callahan's focus is on the problem of moving from a personal right to die according to one's wishes to allowing a physician or any other person to take the life of a patient who requests it. As he explains, "Voluntary euthanasia . . . can only be called 'consenting adult killing.' By that term I mean the killing of one person by another in the name of their mutual right to be killer and killed if they freely agree to play those roles" (Callahan 1992, 52).

Although this seems awkwardly expressed by Callahan – the idea of moving from my right to die to another's right to kill – I take his issue to be that it is never morally acceptable for a person to take on the obligation to help a patient die even when that desire is expressed and adjudicated. In fact, as recently as 2002 he says as much (Callahan 2002, 53). It is clear that any particular person may decline to assist, but should it be allowable for someone, anyone, to accept the responsibility?[15] Terminally ill patients are often in highly compromised situations that demand the aid of others. The problem, it seems to me, is that the question here is not one of "rights" (i.e.,

---

[15] Other possible interpretations of Callahan's statement are easily dismissed, I believe, as either obviously uninteresting or not morally complex enough to address at this time. For example, it is ridiculous to believe that physicians or "lay people" have been given a "right" to kill, if by this we mean that they can go around killing without impediment or consequence simply because we have also accepted as a society the "right to die." A "right to die" clearly does not warrant unconsented-to acts of killing. Further, if we simply mean that society has sanctioned the right of a doctor to kill a patient, this is still all predicated on the patient's desire to die, which is clearly a relationship of rights to obligations, not rights to rights.

"permissions" or "allowances") as Callahan asks it, but instead it is a question of what morality *requires* of those of us who are part of the lives of dying patients: What *should we do* when a dying patient asks for our help? Particularly in cases of assisted suicide and euthanasia, others are asked to participate in securing the means to the patient's desired ends because the patient is unable to carry out the task by herself. Of course, these requests can simply be ignored; however, that neither makes them go away nor does it rule out complicity since the expressed desires of the patient now exist within the fabric of the situation, obligating others to adjudicate these claims over and against other concrete claims and obligations.

It is just such an adjudication of claims and their corresponding obligations that we discussed at length in Chapter 3, and we discovered that contrary to Callahan's implications, there is nothing magical in a move from rights to duty, from one's claim to another's obligation. This connection between claims and obligations is simply part and parcel of social interaction when individuals express their desires to and with others. This is certainly no less true in the medical arena at the bedside of a terminally ill patient. Given contemporary technology, given current suffering, given the lack of physical abilities in this patient, given a "terminal" diagnosis, given this patient's voice asking to die, what are we to do? We are, it seems clear, to assess reasonably her claim in the complex of her personal, medical situation and our own standing obligations. And given the vast number of different patient situations, it should not be surprising to find that we are not only initially but on reflection – that is, "ethically" – obligated[16] to help *some* particular terminally ill patients die.

More central to my argument than even these issues, however, is my use of the terms "significance" and "meaning." One of Callahan's primary concerns with euthanasia is that he cannot understand why

---

[16] As is clear from the previous chapter, this obligation does not follow from a "right" *per se*, but only from the claims of patients upon the adjudication of their corresponding obligations that compete for our moral attention. Thus, the obligation differs from other arguments in favor of an obligation for PAS, in that many of those move from a right of self-determination to such an obligation (cf. Battin 2005, especially ch. 4).

anyone would believe that she could find meaning through killing herself. He contends that "people commit suicide because they find life empty, oppressive, or meaningless" and goes on to imply that euthanasia is medicine's only response to the meaninglessness of life felt by some terminally ill patients (Callahan 1992, 55). In the essay "When Abstract Moralizing Runs Amok," John Lachs replies to Callahan:[17]

It is grotesque to suppose that they [the terminally ill] are looking for the meaning of existence and find it, absurdly, in a lethal injection. Their predicament is not intellectual but existential. They are interested not in seeking the meaning of life but in acting on their belief that their own continued existence is, on balance, of no further benefit to them. (Lachs 1994, 10)

At first, this claim seems to strike directly at the heart of my contention that euthanasia can be an act of meaning for some individuals. However, with only a little reflection, this statement can be seen to support rather than to refute my argument. Here Lachs is directly attacking Callahan's contention concerning the relationship between "meaning" and acts of dying through suicide or euthanasia. But both authors – Callahan directly and Lachs in his "echo" of Callahan – use the term "meaning" far too abstractly for our purposes. As a matter of fact, this is precisely Lachs's problem with Callahan's argument. Surely, as Lachs points out, it is absurd to see lethal injection as *the* answer to the mystery of life. We do not *find* meaning through euthanasia, as if meaning is to be discovered, out there; terminal illness is an "existential" problem that must be confronted by existential, not transcendental, solutions. It has already been argued that meaning is an everyday thing to be created and formed through our own powers; it arises from our intellectual wellspring of ideals, and culminates in progressive activity that courageously pursues those ideals we deem fitting for our life processes as they are and as we wish them to be.

For someone to consider her existence to be "on balance, of no further benefit" is correspondingly to consider that meaning can no

---

[17] Callahan (1994) has his own response to Lachs that follows Lachs's article in the same journal.

longer be gained by pursuing activities that are intended to further living. Here, then, the final process of dying comes into focus, and meaning can be given to it by our considered activities to secure a controlled, significant death. The meaning is not so much in the instrument(s) used to reach the goal of death nor in the goal itself; it is found in the *complete* act of pursuing our reasoned ends, in the combination of means and ends, instruments and goals.[18]

It is clear, though, that choices surrounding dying processes are based, no doubt, on grim options, and they may come down to trying to provide for the terminally ill what Margaret Battin calls "the least worst death" (see Battin 1994). However, I have attempted to put a more positive spin on human interactions concerning issues of death and dying. I believe there are real occasions where it is not only permissible but morally important to aid the dying on their own terms when their desires are "intelligently conceived" and wed to appropriate means at our disposal. This aid provides the opportunity for active participation and the exercise of personal desires culminating in a significant death – that is, dying meaningfully. Avoiding this realization and ignoring the pleas of the dying can indeed be morally tragic.

The Place of Palliative Care and Hospice

Before concluding this chapter, I want to say a word about the rise and ethical use of palliative care and hospice. Palliative care, it must be acknowledged, is a form of aid in dying that should be available to every patient.[19] Hospice and other institutional palliative

---

[18] I have been careful not to argue about *how* we are to help the dying. This may be objectionable to some who might say that euthanizing practices are always objectionable but assistance in suicide may be allowable. However, the meaning of our actions and aid are best determined in particular cases within the narratives of patients themselves. I hope I have made clear that I do not see any reasons to rule out either kind of practice *a priori*.

[19] In fact, Joseph Fins' book *A Palliative Ethic of Care* (2006) explains well what palliative medicine can and should be. If such care were readily available in all hospitals and other medical institutions in the United States, I suspect that the call for PAS and other forms of aid in dying would be greatly reduced. Further, Fins' focus on

developments in end-of-life care are often explicitly set forth in opposition to the kinds of assistance mentioned, and supported by the arguments presented earlier. Further, the ethical importance of palliative care, when seen as a morally stronger alternative to other forms of aid in dying, varies depending on patient populations to which such a general claim is applied (in fact, I will argue in Chapter 6 that palliative care with children [as a population] has significantly stronger moral warrant than with adults [as a population]). Finally, as noted at the end of Chapter 4, neither PAS nor euthanasia need even arise as "live options" for patients *if* the environment in which their dying occurs succeeds in offering them the kind of care, dignity, and respect necessary to satisfy their meaningful activities in the dying process.

While palliative measures and hospice care have been available in limited setting for well over twenty years, even today many institutions are lacking adequate resource for palliative aid for their dying patients. The AMA itself recognized the deplorable lack of good education in end-of-life care, and so in the late 1990s came out with its EPEC (Education on Palliative and End-of-Life Care) training material, which it distributed on CD-ROM to all its members. Meanwhile, many studies have shown the positive effects for many patients that follow from good palliative and hospice care, where both excellent pain management and careful psychosocial support provides dying persons with the mechanisms necessary to make their dyings meaningful to them.

Philosophically, palliative care has been described as a "whole-person" approach primarily aimed at compassionate end-of-life care for an individual patient (Foley 2002). This approach focuses on the care of the patient, mentally and physically as a result of her consent (Randall & Downie 1999). Alternately, some have described hospice as a community-oriented approach that treats patients as importantly related to others where dying is not a solitary act whose burdens must

---

"goals of care" is an excellent corrective to (or, better yet, proactive avoidance of) seeming conflict between healthcare professionals and patients/families. I will say more about this in later chapters.

be born alone by the patient. As Ira Byock has argued, hospice is covenantal where "the connection to community cannot be severed. Within a covenantal approach to illness – caregiving, dying, and grief – people respond to others out of a sense of mutuality and because they are motivated by a desire to care" (Byock 2003, S40).

However, Foley, Byock, and others have argued that hospice and other similar palliative initiatives, both as compassionate and as communal, are direct alternatives to intentional acts of dying (Foley 2002; Byock 2003; cf. Stoddard 1991). In particular, it is the seemingly individualistic character of acts such as PAS, described as self-concerned, that creates the stark juxtaposition. Three things need to be said in response.

First, there is no doubt that hospice offers many patients a viable alternative in their last months of life. Further, should our medical, psychological, financial, and socio-political acts and instruments that surround and support palliative care for dying patients continue to improve, there is reason to hope that fewer and fewer requests for other forms of aid in dying will be made (cf. Quill and Battin 2004, specifically 323–33).

Second, I have been arguing that beyond those patients who would be well-served by palliative care and hospice there are some people for whom even this alternative is not what is most meaningful, dignified, "best" – whether Ms. K. be the paradigm, or some other suffering patients with bones so brittle they can break performing simple, everyday movements or patients who respond poorly or are allergic to drug therapy. Put more poetically in the words of John McDermott, this is not about cowardice or rashness; it is about "persons for whom the nectar has gone permanently sour and for whom the door of amelioration has been locked" (McDermott 2006, 254). In these (again, hopefully few) cases, the argument that our assistance in helping support or provide means to fulfilling that meaning is morally defensible stands.[20]

---

[20] See Quill, Lee, and Nunn (2002) for presentations of case studies that identify different features that might lead to offering different end-of-life care options based on the extent to which they consider minimizing harm.

Third, it is the basic contention of this book that no one is an isolated individual, and even the most individualistic acts have deep communal connections. We must investigate carefully both the affects of such decisions on others and how others affect the decision. Undue, even unwitting, pressure can be brought to bear on dying individuals, and yet we need only look at the cases of Ms. K. and Ramon from Chapter 1 to see how such decisions involve and affect more than just an individual patient. Often the fact that the desire for PAS is made precisely in consideration of and with others is what makes it a morally viable possibility for those who seek it.

Conclusion

As human beings, we will die, but *how* we die is yet to be determined for each one of us. That we might wish to have some control over the dying process is neither inappropriate nor unusual. Living a meaningful life, including the process of dying, is both desirable and laudable provided we take to heart the fact that true meaning comes through intelligent activity. For some terminally ill patients, human dignity and significant living lie not in an ability to see the body as a biological apparatus that can, through mechanical measures, be kept alive, but instead in recognizing the fact that the meaning of a life comes from the activity of fusing virtues with ideals, adjusting means and ends to each other, in order to shape the outcome of our participation in the world.

Within a consistently significant life, problems concerning death rarely arise. At the end of significance is the abyss facing the terminally ill patient. It is up to the patient to decide to progress toward death, or to fight it off. The arguments in this chapter attempt to make clear that significant human living does not have to end with a diagnosis of terminal illness, and that there are no legitimate reasons *a priori* to condemn all acts of euthanasia and assisted suicide. In very real, deeply painful, tragic, and, yes, loving situations, those who do not engage patients who are suffering and who request to die do so at a great cost, for they fail to fulfill their obligations. Situated, social beings must thoughtfully adjudicate patients' requests to die.

When genuine, sincere, and thorough reflection has occurred, we will find that there will be morally legitimate occasions for these acts, and within a community we will help provide meaning to a dying person's last living moments, thereby helping empower the patient as narrator of her own complete life story.

5

Experiencing Lost Voices

Dying without Capacity

> [M]ost patients ... [dying without decisional capacity] are incomplete persons in need of fabrication by others. This is a place of medical treatment that contains a crucial absence – of patients emplaced in embodied lives. .
>
> *Sharon Kaufman*

Chapter 4 focused on those patients who, though in the midst of dying processes, are able to participate in decision making regarding their lived experiences of dying. The interests of adult, lucid patients with decisional capacity are at least as varied as there are patients themselves. Further, our own relationship to these patients, our roles and abilities, as well as our knowledge and concern, when carefully considered in light of patient needs and circumstances, may need to be brought to bear on behalf of easing their dying. So, we should not be surprised to find that for some patients, morality requires us to aid them in dying, not simply through passive support but through active application of our skills and roles in their lives and society.

This chapter turns to a different set of patients – namely, those unable to make direct, concurrent decisions about their care in dying. This set of patients does not form a monolithic, homogenous group, and in fact will be viewed under several different kinds of conditions and characterizations.

In 2004, according to the CDC, approximately two-thirds of all deaths in the United States occurred in medically related institutions – hospitals, mostly, but also nursing homes and in-patient hospice settings. Of these, nearly 70 percent of the patients[1] resided in what sociologists call "total institutions," where around the clock patients' lives are circumscribed not only by the walls but also by the routines, employees, and policies of the institutions in which they reside (cf. Kamerman 1988, 40–53). Such "totalizing" places patients into significantly different environments from ones they are used to, putting them within institutions controlled by rules and practices not always of their own desire or choosing, cutting them off from their traditional supportive environments.

However, while Chapter 4 discussed patients who, depending on their illness or injury, may or may not be confined to a "total institution" for the duration of their dying processes, in virtually all cases the same cannot be said for the kinds of patients addressed by this chapter – those who have severe decisional compromise. In fact, not only are the patients discussed in this chapter typically confined to medical institutions, but their very ability to speak for themselves is so highly compromised (if not entirely absent) that others will be left to make decisions for and about them. In this way, not only the environments but the habits that traditionally operate in those environments to express their sense of self are lost to these patients. Thus, *others* (surrogates, family, friends, physicians, social workers, etc.) are often challenged to determine ethically appropriate actions that will lead to appropriate dying processes *for* these patients.

While there is a certain overlap of the ethical issues, several important differences among patients will be discussed in this chapter. On the one hand, there are patients who are "permanently" unconscious, unable because of injury or extremes of disease to *inter*act with the world around them – these are patients who are brain dead or in a permanent vegetative state. On the other hand, there are neurologically compromised patients whose decision-making abilities have declined as disease or degeneration has ravaged their brains.

---

[1] Some patients counted as "hospital" deaths were pronounced dead on arrival, and others were in out-patient, not in-patient, hospital settings.

Permanent Decisional Incapacity[2]

The end of the twentieth century saw the ability of medicine to keep the hearts and lungs of patients working, and to feed patients through surgically inserted tubes. These technological advances brought new cases and concerns to medical ethics, as patients who have severe neurological impairment that has destroyed their decisional capacity and even, in the most extreme cases, their ability to have experiences, now languish in medical institutions. Drawing on law and ethics, two seminal cases occurred in the late-twentieth century (Karen Ann Quinlan 1975–6 and Nancy Cruzan 1983–90) and the beginning of the twenty-first century brought us the trials and tribulations of Terri Schiavo and Terry Wallis. These cases raise serious ethical questions about surrogate decision making at the end of life. But in order to understand the issues raised, it will help to describe the multiple conditions in which patients may find themselves that will raise ethical concerns about and for surrogacy.

As we noted, the condition of "permanent" decision-making incapacitation is characterized by the inability of patients to communicate about, understand, and make important decisions concerning their own well-being. While there remain legitimate empirically problematic questions about the permanence of the conditions of these patients, we shall discuss primarily two different types of (suppositionally) permanently incapacitated patients: those who are brain dead and those in persistent/permanent vegetative states (PVS).

Brain Death

"Brain-dead," said the doctor. "There is no chance that he will wake up. Ever. Look here." And he rolled a scroll of paper onto her lap.

"This is the electroencephalograph. It's nothing but a flat line. No blips." Hannah bowed her head over the chart. The doctor cleared his throat, took one of her hands in both of his, and leaned toward her as though about to tell a secret. Hannah submitted to what under any other circumstances she might have considered presumption, submitted because she

---

[2] This section started with material from Hester 1998, but has been revised extensively in light of the new world of neurological findings regarding brain death, PVS, MCS, and other conditions.

thought she ought to. It was expected of her. The formality of the occasion and all.

"Hannah, it is three weeks since your husband was shot in the head. The only thing keeping him alive is the respirator."

Hannah waited for the walls of the solarium to burst.

"I'm asking you to let us put an end to it, unplug the machinery, let him go. There is just no sense in prolonging a misfortune." Hannah felt that she should say something, not just sit there, but for the life of her she couldn't think what. . . . (Selzer 1990, 3–4)

Brain death – depending on criteria used, aka "whole central nervous system," "whole brain," "brain stem," death by neurological criteria, or "neocortical" death; cf. Facco and Machado 2004 – is, in a very broad sweep, intended to indicate the neurological condition of no activity[3] throughout the brain. Or according to the 1981 President's Commission, it is the "irreversible cessation of all functions of the entire brain, including the brain stem" (73). Neither conscious activity nor reflexive motor response occurs. One confirmatory indicator of this is that the patient shows no functional electrical activity within the brain when connected to an electroencephalogram (EEG), after other clinical indicators such as atropine and apnea testing have been performed (Lang and Heckman 2004). In brain death, pulmonary function can often be maintained by medical machinery even while cardiac function continues, since the pumping of the heart is a largely independent bodily function. Though brain death was described in the medical literature as early as 1959, it was only with the Harvard Committee on Brain Death (1968, 337–340) and later the President's Commission (1981, 60–84) that brain death became accepted both as a medical and legal criterion for death – supported both by the American Medical Association and in law.

But even given this history, both the determination *and* use of "brain death" has proven controversial. "Death" itself has long been discussed by philosophers and scientists, and the "addition" of "brain

---

[3] This is not uncontroversial (as we will see), with some endocrine and other functions, and even spontaneous bodily movements, still occurring. See Wijdicks 2001 for a review of the literature on "brain death."

death" in 1968 as a form of death to be considered not only by philosophers (cf. Jonas 1974; Veatch 1976; 2005; Potts 2001; Lizza 2004; 2005; Seifert 2004; Kipnis 2004) but by physicians and policy experts has, even to this day, in no way cleared up the issue (e.g., Truog 1997; Shewmon 1998, 2001; Potts et al. 2000; Halevy 2001; Karakatsanis and Tsanakas 2002; Hughes 2004; Shewmon and Shewmon 2004; President's Council 2009). For example, some argue about the "true" medical status of a brain-dead individual. On the one hand, many neurologists, neurobiologists, and ethicists accept that death occurs when certain physiological conditions obtain (or are absent) in the brain – including the cortex, cerebellum, stem, and so on (cf. Korein and Machado 2004). On the other hand, the criteria for those conditions seem unsettled (multiple standards exist; Byrne and Weaver 2004, 44–45), unclear (the meaning and requirements of those standards are at times vague; Byrne and Weaver 2004, 45–46), even nonexistent (e.g., "irreversibility," it is argued, is an empirically unfoundable criterion; Byrne and Weaver 2004, 47–48; cf. Bernat 2004). Furthermore, many biological and physiological processes continue in persons pronounced "brain dead" – including endocrine functions, electrocerebral activity, and even spinal responses (Karakatsanis and Tsanakas 2002). Still others claim that we have rushed into accepting questionable criteria for the determination of death because the relationship between brain death and organ procurement for transplantation is so intimate (brain death is a legally accepted requirement for the donation of organs – Jonas 1974, Kerridge et al. 2002; Rappaport and Rappaport 2004). There are cultural and religious objections to any account of death based solely on brain-based criteria (e.g., Rosner 1999).[4]

As Robert Veatch (1999), Alexander Capron (1999; 2001) and others have rightly pointed out, determining death has specific legal and moral implications concerning the existence of certain rights, and with so much depending on the criteria applied to determine brain death, we would do well not to lose track of the consequences

---

[4] There are more objection-types, and reviews of the different kinds of arguments and claims surrounding brain death can be found in Dagi and Kaufman 2001, Veatch 2005, and President's Council 2009.

of extreme neurological compromise for those afflicted. I will not attempt to adjudicate all these conflicts surrounding brain death. I am no neurologist, nor am I particularly focused on specific legal consequences (save for how they affect and are affected by the moral issues). As illustrated by the December 2008 "white paper" on the determination of death from the President's Council on Bioethics (2009), it is clear that these issues are in no way settled (related confusion, perhaps even more strongly evidenced, will be noted when discussing PVS later).[5] And yet, as pointed out by Younger and Arnold, "Brain death has been 'grandfathered' into public acceptance and . . . is unlikely to be rejected because of its theoretical imperfections" (2001, 533). What I think is most important, then, is to investigate the moral implications for the caregivers and decision makers of these patients (or, if one prefers, these "dead persons"). And while this cannot be divorced from the question of whether or not the patient is "in fact" dead, the more processive account of death and dying that we have been operating under throughout this book makes the "fact" of death (as a moment or static condition) less pronounced than how we act in the case of a patient whose medical condition clearly places her in the midst of a process of dying.

In this light, then, debates about "irreversibility" begin to sound like squabbles over our technical abilities to (ever) pronounce with such certainty. However, it is a truism that no such certainty exists in medicine – or anywhere else in life, for that matter. Our need to discover criteria for "absolute" death are clearly in vain, and some idea of "functional" death is more appropriate to lived experience. This is not to say that it matters little whether or not we pronounce "irreversibility" (value-laden as the idea obviously is), but the question here is what *does* depend on our use of brain death, functional death,

---

[5] We can point to the story of Zach Dunlap (twenty-one-year-old in an ATV accident), as an example of the continued confusions that surround brain-death declarations. Zach was pronounced "brain dead" on November 19, 2007, and was being prepped for organ retrieval when a pocket knife that scraped across his foot "woke him up." The hospital claimed "faulty equipment" for the misdiagnosis. The family claims that this was a result of divine intervention. Either way, the story adds to the medical, cultural, and philosophical confusions surrounding brain death declarations. See http://news.yahoo.com/s/ap/20080324/ap_on_fe_st/not_dead;_ylt=Aky1O4oJaayIs2zEujyr6n2soNUE, among other sites, for the story.

as a medically pronounceable condition of human beings?[6] One response is apparent: Social and cultural practices become triggered by pronouncements of death. While we may differ on the significance and characterization of some of these, I appreciate Veatch's emphasis on the "death behaviors" as part of the very meaning of "death" (1976; 2005).

On the one hand, when brain death is determined by a physician medically – that is, *death* according to that physician and to the legal system – the moral implication is that medicine has no further obligation to treat (which I distinguish from "care for" and "care about" – an obligation that continues) the patient who has so been declared brain dead. This is clearly a significant moral fact. The questions to ask ourselves are then: Is *any* possibility for "reversibility" enough to cease the use of such a definition? Should we accept this kind of unilateral determination of obligations toward patients from physicians?

While the "death point" is still debatable by those who hold an absolute obligation to sustain life or, at least, its possibilities, it is clear that death-point identification is not always possible, and since dying is a process, identifying the actual death point is not always morally necessary.[7] For example, we see, rightly I would argue, in the practice of CPR that cessation of medical intervention is reasonable after sufficient evidence is offered that CPR is "futile"[8] in

---

[6] Again, to be clear, this is *not* to claim that nothing practical or important turns on our *definition* of "death," especially as long as we hold strictly to the so-called "dead donor rule" for procuring transplantable organs and tissue (a topic not central to the discussion here, but important to many families as part of end-of-life considerations). This *is* to claim, however, that the definition of death should play a less vital role in end-of-life considerations than should the trajectory of the dying process in light of the patient's life story.

[7] This take on the matter would fall under the critique by Dagi and Kaufman (2001) of the "as if" arguments concerning "brain death," where brain death is to be treated "as if" it is death (implying that it is not "in fact" death). My point is not that it is not "in fact" death; it is simply death from the perspective of medicine. It may not be death from the perspective of other cultural institutions or even specific individuals, but that fact need not burden medical professionals with obligations to provide specific treatment options.

[8] I use this word cautiously as I do not wish to open (though I probably do regardless) the Pandora's box of the debate concerning "medical futility," but a minimal definition of "futile" ("it doesn't serve its intended purpose") would apply here. For contrasting accounts of the "futility" issue, see Rubin 1998 and Schneiderman and Jecker 1995. For a collection of essays on the topic, see Zucker/Zucker 1997.

restarting a sustainable heartbeat. However, can anyone say that the next CPR attempt would not succeed? Of course not; but reasonable efforts need not include eternal obligation. The finitude of human lives, intelligence, and fortitude should not be taken as the un-ideal conditions that limit the ideal world. Instead, as we saw with William James's take on "meaning" and "significance" in life, they should be seen as *our* world's conditions for which the ideals we develop *must* account. What this entails is that conditions, carefully defined according to the current conditions of medicine and society, may be determined that establish the limits of our obligations to others.

What follows is that certain obligations for the medical staff may cease, while some unilateral decisions might be accepted. As Halevy and Brody (1993) state, and put succinctly later by Brody:

> But don't we have to identify a specific point in time at which the organism died? Aren't there important questions which need to be answered and can only be answered by identifying the precise point in the process at which the organism died? These questions include when life support [any "treatment"] can unilaterally (without patient or surrogate concurrence) be withdrawn, when organs can be harvested, and when the organism can be buried or cremated. Perhaps not.... Perhaps these questions need to be examined and answered each on its own.... (1999, 79)

Further, it is unreasonable to expect medical professionals to be obligated for continuing care of some patients. "Brain death," while still controversial, would seem to be well characterized as a circumstance in which the patient's condition (whatever the important diagnostic nuances) signals the end of the physician's obligations.

Of course, an important concern here is the fear of abuse of the "unilateral" power of physicians to determine brain death. This is a legitimate concern. And yet, along with William Gavin, we note, that "death does not have meaning invariance." It is, however, restricted to "social categories, not individual ones" (1995, 55). Thus "death" as a social concept, and not one merely reducible to some physiological "fact" nor open to individual pronouncements outside a cultural context, means that the development of standards and the checks-and-balances of legislation, litigation, and social review are tools that can well equip us against abuse. The alternative, it would seem, is clearly unacceptable – namely, thousands of bodies lying in hospital beds with no life to be lived, a truly undignified state to exist in.

To follow up this argument, I want to make a paradoxical and (at the same time) obvious point (sometimes it is good to remind ourselves of the obvious): While arguable standards do exist to determine brain death, and state laws that make brain death a legally accepted diagnosis do exist, standards and laws should not replace good ethical reflection. Careful diagnostic procedures must *always* be implemented. "Sloppiness" has been blamed for a great many poorly diagnosed cases of brain death (for example, see the case of Zach Dunlap, fn 5), and this "sloppiness" is itself an overt moral failing. Furthermore, clear, complete, and metered communication with surrogates is necessary to make sure that all parties have a reasonable understanding of the situation of the patient. Finally, while we might question whether any "self" still exists, a radically empirical approach to the narrative self that is (was) this patient demands that her death be viewed in light of her life. In particular, if religio-cultural issues are central to the life story of the patient, and those issues exclude brain death as an acceptable criterion for death (e.g., in Orthodox Judaism), we are hard pressed to ignore this in lieu of medical standards and the law. It simply is not obvious *prima facie* that an individual deeply integrated with her Orthodox beliefs should have to lose "treatment," ignoring the significance of her beliefs. Again, here we have expressed claims calling out for our recognition, and these claims can be interpreted to imply that patient interests trump.

But we must be cautious here. The narrative self is not atomic and insular. Patient interests not only arise from some context, but must be adjudicated within a larger community of interests. Thus, the *de facto* obligation that comes with expressed patient interests only becomes morally appropriate to follow *after* a consideration of them with other obligations relevant to the situation – obligations raised, for example, by distributive justice concerns for scarce resources. Further, any adjudication of interests and obligations must, in its most practical moments, identify who is to be burdened by any identified *moral* obligation. Thus, even if some obligations to a patient's religious or cultural values exist, this does not mean that physicians *qua* physicians are obligated to provide therapies that are otherwise deemed medically inappropriate. If "brain death" diagnoses (carefully made with medical, cultural, and legal oversight as mentioned) denote a value statement about physician obligations, what this may mean is not that medicine must accommodate cultural claims about the status of brain death, but that other financial, cultural, religious, and governmental institutions must do so.

Furthermore, whether the controversies surrounding brain death can be settled, even if only within the specific surrogate/family/provider relationship, where the acceptance of criteria to determine that no adequate level of physiological activity in the brain persists for human life to exist (in much the same way that our culture views cardio-pulmonary responses – that is, the biological condition of brain death is *death*), this would not eliminate all practical, ethical concerns. For if brain death is death, then it requires of us practices that support such a definition, and these are practices not currently operative in many medical settings. For example, it is common, as in the scene with Hannah earlier, for physicians, upon diagnosis of brain death, to ask family members whether or not they wish to cease medical treatment. While I will say more about surrogate decision making later, this would, at first glance, seem unproblematic. However, it is not uncommon for families to request that treatment continue. Such a request puts physicians in an ethical bind – the patient is dead and yet treatment (costly and limited) continues. It is important to see, however, that this is a bind of their own making, for if brain death is death, then no *decision* about treatment need be made and therefore no decision from the family need be requested (cf. Capron 2001).

Let me reiterate that making such a statement about our practices in one direction need not imply much about our practices in another. That is, not asking the family what to do need not entail offering the family no closure. Offering the family the opportunity to spend time at their loved one's side, allowing them either to be present or not when respiratory and other support ceases, giving them time to come in from various parts of the country, and so on are acceptable, laudable, even morally required options to be pursued, and yet none of them entails treating the patient as anything other than dead.

Vegetative States

One implication of the controversies surrounding "brain death" diagnoses is that physicians are faced not with a dead patient but with a living one. As such, their obligations to care and treat the patient continue. I have argued otherwise, stating that even though the controversies exist and persist, a diagnosis of "brain death" need not indicate that the "death point" has been reached, but that the condition the patient is in no longer requires medicine to continue with its technologies and "life sustaining" services.

However, according to Robert Veatch, the controversies regarding brain death simply further his thirty-year-old argument that value factors other than "pure medicine" are truly at play here, and that if brain death were investigated carefully, a reasonable view would demonstrate that not only "whole brain dead" patients merit unilateral decisions to forego medical intervention; so do "higher-brain dead" patients (1976; 2005). By "higher-brain" dead patients, Veatch means what has come to be called the patient in a "permanent vegetative state" (PVS).[9] There is no question that this position is more problematic both legally and morally.

The "vegetative state" (VS) was first described in 1972 by Jennett and Plum to indicate what the OED calls "a merely physical life . . . capable of growth and development but devoid of sensation and thought." A vegetative state is the condition of the loss of "higher" brain (cerebrum) functions (typically from "lack of blood flow [ischemia] or oxygen [hypoxia]" [Cranford 1988, 28]) while at least some of the "lower" brain (brain stem) functions remain intact. The higher brain is the seat of awareness and consciousness while the brain stem "controls vegetative functions, such as respiration, and primitive stereotyped reflexes, such as the pupillary response to light" (Cranford 1988, 27). A vegetative state may begin in a coma that lasts a few weeks to several months, but when the patients comes out of the coma, is characterized by an "eyes-open unconsciousness" (Cranford 1988, 28). Patients can often breathe on their own, and sometimes react involuntarily to loud noises or other sharp stimuli.

---

[9] I will reserve the acronym PVS for "permanent" not "persistent" vegetative states, as these are defined by the Multi-Society Task Force (1994).

This condition can last anywhere from a few months to years. A few PVS patients have actually survived more than thirty-five years in this condition, and ending[10] in complete biological death. To be clear, and according to the 1994 Multi-Society Task Force working on issues surrounding PVS, the "condition" alluded to is a vegetative state, with the addition of the adjective "persistent" used to designate a situation in which the *current* vegetative condition persists for more than one month but less than three months. If the condition persists for more than three months *and* the condition's root cause was an anoxic event, then the adjective "permanent" is used; if, however, the condition was caused by a traumatic event, the condition must persist more than twelve months before it can be considered "permanent."[11] P(ermanent)VS, correctly diagnosed, is considered to be irreversible. More precisely, the standard position is that an anoxic event (as is seen in the Multi-Society guidelines) is a better predictor of the "permanence" of PVS than trauma.[12]

In the case of brain death, legally (and, I contend, morally), little question concerning the nature of a meaningful dying process or euthanasia arises because the patient is dead. However, the case of a PVS patient is more problematic.

Medically, there is a great deal of controversy over PVS diagnoses. What makes PVS such a troubling condition for prognostic pronouncement is that its diagnosis is still in question. At the same time, the parameters of our understanding of neurophysiology

[10] More and more is appearing in the literature about PVS patients who "come out" of PVS into some other condition – typically a "minimally conscious state" (MCS) (a review of PVS versus MCS diagnoses is given by Wijdkicks & Cranford 2005).

[11] It is important to emphasize the neurophysiological differences that occur when VS stems from trauma vs. anoxia (see Schiff et al. 2002). Once again, though, these definitions are not uncontroversial (cf. Shewmon 2004, 226).

[12] While PVS should not be confused with chronic comatose or other neurological conditions where higher-brain functions may still be intact even though little to no response is forthcoming from the patient for weeks, months, or even years at a time, much has been written, particularly in Britain, concerning the "misdiagnosis" of PVS. See Andrews et al. 1996, Ramsay 1996, and Zeman 1997. Furthermore, arguments have been put forth to drop the "permanent" qualifier since, like the "irreversibility" qualifier for "brain death," permanence is not an empirically verifiable condition (cf. Laureys et al. 2004).

continue to shift, as seen in the publication of two different articles (2006) that raised direct questions about our understanding
of PVS.

The first was an article in the little known journal *NeuroRehabilitation*, where the authors, Clauss and Nel (2006), reported three
patients in diagnosed PVS were temporarily "aroused" with the help
of a 10 mg dose of zolpidem (aka Ambien) – a medication typically
taken as a sleep aid – with each patient demonstrating intentional
interaction with their environments (from laughing at television to
conversing with family). This finding comes as a result of long-term
use of zolpidem by these two physicians in several different kinds
of patients with neurological compromises (2000). However, since
neither investigator is a board certified neurologist (one is a nuclear
medicine specialist, the other a family practice physician), there is at
least some reason to suspect that the initial diagnosis of PVS in these
cases may have been mistaken. And yet the authors claim to have followed the Multi-Society Taskforce guidelines (1994) for diagnosis.
So, given the results with zolpidem, either there was a misdiagnosis
of PVS, and thus the authors would have been mistaken about what
had occurred, or it was correct, in which case the implications of a
diagnosis of PVS would no longer carry the prognostic force that was
intended.

The second article (Owen et al. 2006) made an even more significant impact on the medical scene. Publishing in the well-known
journal *Science*, neurological researchers demonstrated with the use
of functional magnetic resonance imaging (fMRI) that the brain of
a particular female patient diagnosed in a VS (starting five months
after severe brain trauma) showed distinct electrical activity when
given commands – specifically commands concerning playing tennis
and moving through her house. This research followed on the heels
of the authors' previous work from 2002 that demonstrated cerebral responses by PVS patients to the use of the patients' names. The
claims of the authors beyond the data remain controversial, however,
as they use such descriptors as "[the patient's] decision to cooper-
ate with the authors by imagining particular tasks when asked to do
so represents a clear act of intention." As pointed out by Naccache
(2006) in a commentary in the same issue, such a conclusion implies
consciousness, and yet other behavioral facts (or lack thereof) do not

support the conclusion. Having said this, there is no doubt that the data itself (while yet to be replicated and its implications fully developed and accepted) may prove significant.[13]

In general, therefore, since PVS patients do not meet the legal definition for declaring them dead and since they may in fact have crude awareness, the decision to continue treating and feeding them is complicated. Unilateral decision making by physicians has less medical support than for those diagnosed as "brain dead." While some argue that there can never exist medical diagnostic procedures to indicate "loss of consciousness," no one argues that those diagnosed as "brain dead" have even "crude consciousness" (alertness or wakefulness). However, the stories of "waking former" PVS patients,[14] and the findings of the fMRI researchers, leads us to question whether or not PVS is irreversible or whether or not some form of consciousness still exists in PVS patients.

The relational and moral difficulty is that PVS patients can neither speak nor act for themselves, and yet there is some form of bodily integrity left in which various biological processes continue in such a way as to retain at least (and maybe more than) reflexive activity. However, given the extreme neurological compromise, some argue[15] that PVS patients no longer embody experienceable and expressible emotions, values, interests, ideals, and virtues. Therefore we are faced with the very real possibility that PVS patients are much like (whole) brain dead individuals; they are already functionally dead. As Tristram Engelhardt recognizes:

However emotionally difficult it will be to take these steps to new understandings, they will be unavoidable, in that it will not be possible generally to justify holding higher-brain-centers-dead but otherwise alive human bodies to be persons. They are not persons. If one kills such an entity, one does not take the life of a person. (Engelhardt 1986, 242)

---

[13] Use of fMRI to identify any existing cerebral networks was also used by Kobylarz & Schiff (2004). They did limited comparisons between PVS and MCS patients, and counter to the suggested implications of Owens et al. Kobylarz and Schiff suggest that fMRI may allow for a clearer conceptual separation between PVS and MCS patients.

[14] There are several examples in the literature: Childs and Mercer 1996, Andrews et al. 1996, and more recently Avesani et al. 2006.

[15] For example, Veatch, Engelhardt, Cranford, and others.

Engelhardt's is a firm stance that trades off the idea of personhood and its connection to higher-brain functioning. But again, whether or not PVS patients are indeed permanently compromised such that they are no longer "persons" is precisely one question that concerns bioethics. Some argue that in cases of PVS, when a health professional discontinues treatment (feeding, intubation, and so on) of a PVS patient, she merely releases the body from its technological bonds. However, others are concerned that it is the surrogates and doctors who in fact kill the patient, rather than the anoxic or traumatic event that earlier befell the patient. The strongest claim concerning obligations to keep PVS patients alive is summed up well by Bobby Schindler (brother of Terry Schiavo): "If a person becomes incapacitated, is not dying, and can assimilate food and water via a feeding tube, then I believe that we are morally obligated to care for the person and provide them this basic care – regardless of . . . what that person's wishes might be" (quoted in *The New Scientist*, March 13, 2007). And yet how can it be that in the case of this most severe neurological compromise, a patient's wishes (whether in the form of a written advance directive or as an extension of her values through her life stories) are not determinative? Surely if life is of value (and presumably that is the reason that such a strong obligation is claimed to exist), it is of value because it is the life *of someone* – a being with interests and values; her interests simply *must* matter.

Either way, what is true *de facto* is that by lacking decision-making capacity, the medical decisions for a PVS patient must be given over to a proxy, or "surrogate decision maker." Given the complexities, the role of the surrogate for PVS patients begins as that of a "watchdog" making sure that thorough evaluation and medical attention has been given. Without any one conclusive technological test, PVS is difficult to diagnose; it has been recommended that though "accurate diagnosis is possible," more than a year should be given, and "a multidisciplinary team experienced in the management of people with complex disabilities" should be allotted to these cases to insure diagnostic accuracy (Andrews et al. 1996, 16). The patient is well served by a surrogate who protects her from hasty conclusions. Thus, a surrogate for a PVS patient should help avoid the possibility of careless misdiagnoses or rash determinations.

Yet what can we say about the PVS patient whose diagnosis is repeatedly confirmed by neurologists, other experts, and technologies? Recall that the radically empirical attitude demands that all experience be taken seriously, and this would seem to require caution with making life-ending decisions for PVS patients who might be experiencing... something. But recall that as a moral fact, radical empiricism comes down to taking interests seriously, and specifically, expressed interests. The challenge with PVS patients, even in the face of fMRI testing, is that there is no way to recognize definitively that what is happening in their brains equates to interests of any clear or meaningful sort.[16] And taking experience seriously does not mean that all *experience* is to be protected and championed, any more than are any and all *interests*. Some interests lead to bad, even evil, ends, and others simply are meaningless (i.e., they never couple with active expression to produce an end result). So, acceptably diagnosed PVS patients may as a matter of moral consequence, as Vetch and others have suggested, begin to move more closely to those who are brain dead than we currently suppose.[17]

Theresa Schindler was a Pennsylvania girl who had struggled with her weight until she determined to lose weight under a physician's care. She succeed in losing 100 pounds, and soon thereafter met the man she would marry, Michael Schiavo, in 1984. By 1990, Terri and Michael were undergoing fertility treatments in order for here to conceive, and her weight continued to drop another 40 pounds.

On February 25, 1990, Terri collapsed in the hallway of the couple's apartment in Florida. Michael immediately called 911 and Terri's parents.

---

[16] To be clear, the fMRI tests do not allow for the conclusion that the patient is conscious or has experiences. While the researchers suggest as much, it is just as reasonable to suppose that what is happening is bare physiological cause-effect mechanisms (from habituated neuron-pathways) with no psychological "awareness" or "intentionality."

[17] Again, Childs and Mercer 1996, Andrews et al. 1996, and others raise questions, but confusion abounds even here, with Childs and Mercer concluding that "permanent vegetative states" are misnomers, while Andrews et al. believe that physicians are simply being too hasty in their diagnoses. The questions here, though, seemed to be raised more for the surrogate in the role of "watchdog" for proper diagnosis and ample time, but not so much so if it can be determined that reasonable diagnosis and waiting have been performed. Some 10,000 + patients languish in hospitals diagnosed in a PVS condition.

A significant myocardial infarction had occurred, leaving Terri's brain without oxygen long enough to cause severe neurological damage. Terri's potassium was severely low, and the cause may have been an eating disorder – bulimia.

Both Michael and Terri's parents worked toward Terri's rehabilitation. In various rehabilitation units, Michael and Terri's mother, Mary, provided care. Formally diagnosed in a persistent vegetative state by the summer of 1990, Michael took Terri to California for experimental brain stimulation. However, a year after the precipitating event, Terri showed no sign of neurological recovery, demonstrating only reflexive responses.

In 1994, Michael began to reconsider whether to continue rehabilitative therapies for Terri. After a successful lawsuit against Terri's obstetrician, with the funds being held in trust for Terri's care, Michael began to discuss end-of-life options for Terri with her physician. It was after this court judgment that the rift between Michael Schiavo and the Schindlers became apparent, with the Schindlers attempting unsuccessfully to remove Michael as Terri's guardian.

It was not until 1997 that Michael finally decided to pursue an order to discontinue life-sustaining treatments, and this was finally entered in May 1998. It was then that the two sides in the battle of Terri became clear and apparent, with Michael claiming that he had lost hope that Terri would recover and the Schindlers affirming that Terri showed signs of "special responses" to Mary Schindler, in particular.[18]

Seven more years of court battles ensued, with numerous neurologists consulted, politicians engaged, media dispatched, and strangers and friends near and far gathered, until Terri finally died after removal of her assisted nutrition and hydration on March 31, 2005.

The situation surrounding Terri Schiavo in 2005 that captivated the media, stimulated the right-to-life movement, energized Congress, bombarded the courts, and confounded medical ethicists is a good case study.

While some dozen physicians who studied Ms. Schiavo declared her to be in a PVS, some people (her parents and Senator Bill Frist among them) believed her to be in what has been called a "minimally conscious" state (MCS). As evidence for the "factual" claim of minimal consciousness, Ms. Schiavo's parents noted that in their

---

[18] Adapted from the report of the John Wolfson, Guardian Ad Litem for Theresa Schivo.

presence she both "smiled" and "grimaced," indicating a certainly level of awareness. Others, too, noted these facial gestures, and so the concern about her diagnosis gained momentum.

Such accounts strike us as moving, even determinative, but in light of the medical evidence in Ms. Schaivo's case, they in fact force us to reconsider the accounts themselves. There is an important conceptual equivocation invoked by the terms "smile" and "grimace," and it may behoove us to clear those up.

Smiling, it has been argued, is a reflexive act arising from particular stimuli. There is an upturn of the lips, a display of teeth, heightening of the cheeks. These physical changes in the face are responses to some cause, and thus speak not only to the one who smiles, but to the cause of that smile. Let us grant this general explanation as sound and valid; the question then is: What is the cause that is implicated?

For the most part, conscious beings smile when pleased – pleased by humor, pleased by tickling or caressing, pleased by music, and so on. These particular pleasures come to the one who smiles from external stimuli. Of course, internal causes may be implicated as well – the memory of a good friend or a pleasurable dream. Whether from internal or external causes, to be pleased, and the reflexive act of smiling that follows, no doubt emanate from a conscious being.

The problem is that the act of turning up one's lips has physiological components that need not be tied to any pleasurable stimuli. My wife can stop me and ask, "Why are you smiling?" and at times I can legitimately answer that I didn't know that I was smiling and that I have no reason for it. But beyond this, a reflexive act, because of its physiological processes, can occur through multiple pathways. The question to be taken on directly then is that if we grant both that Ms. Schiavo smiled and that smiling is stimulated by some cause, was it possible for Ms. Schaivo to smile?

Here the medical facts and the claims of Ms. Schaivo's parents seem to run headlong into each other. If, as the many physicians claim, she was in a PVS, then although PVS patients are capable of a great many reflexive acts because the physiology of nerves and synapses allows for such acts, there would be no way for Ms. Schiavo to do so "intentionally" or "consciously." That is, the upturn of lips is not, itself, a smile. But, maybe this is too simplistic a response by medicine.

Can someone smile yet not be a conscious being? The problem is built into our very concept of a "smile" as the idea that *pleasurable* stimuli (or conscious contortions – as when my son is asked to smile for a picture) must be present. Thus, built into her parents' description of Ms. Schiavo's facial movements was the idea of consciousness itself. And yet there is nothing in the act of upturned lips itself that warrants inclusion of higher-order processes. If a frog's legs can wiggle when electrical current is applied to the nerve even when no head exists, it would seem possible that a severely brain damaged person (and no one contends that Ms. Schiavo was anything other than that) could turn up her lips and show her teeth with nothing more than purely physiological stimuli.

Of course, such a conclusion does not settle the dispute, but it does point out that even the simplest of descriptions are already laden with the values and interests of those doing the describing. They project as much as they report, but the dangers of such projections are multiple and well known.

On July 13th, 1984, Terry Wallis and two of his closes friends went driving through the Ozark Mountains in their home state of Arkansas. No one knows precisely why, but their truck lost control on a back woods road and spun out....

Terry was twenty years old – a lanky, black-haired, fun-loving self-proclaimed hillbilly. When he didn't have half his body stuck under the hood of a car, he was a laughing, dancing, howling Southern sensation. He had his whole life ahead of him. He and his wife Sandi had just welcomed their first child, Amber – six weeks old. But the crash delivered a massive blow to Terry's head. By the time rescuers were able to pull him from the gorge, he had already slipped into a coma.

He was Medevac'd to a nearby hospital, where he lay in bed, silent and still for the next three months. His family stood beside him, waiting. Apart from the head trauma and some minor contusions, Terry was physically fine.... [D]octors issued a cautious preliminary statement: if he emerged from his coma, he had a pretty good chance of recuperating. But would he snap out of it?

The answer came in October of 1984. Terry opened his eyes on his own; he had broken free of the coma. But the doctors' worst fears had been realized. The blow to Terry's head had severely damaged his brain. He was now a vegetative quadriplegic.

Terry's condition confused his family. At times, for instance, he appeared alert; he could grunt and fidget as if irritated with his confinement in bed. His eyes sometimes tracked people who entered his room and he often appeared to understand what was going on around him. If his food was liquefied and spooned into his mouth, he could eat well enough. There were glimpses, in other words, that Terry was still "in there." The family bolstered their hopes.

But doctors cautioned the Wallises. These reactions, they said, were pure illusion.... No matter how convincingly Terry seemed to "be there" every now and then, he was – in fact – utterly incapable of cognition. The doctors made themselves very clear on this point: the man the Wallises had once known as a loving husband and son was gone.

The Wallises never accepted the doctors' diagnosis of Terry's condition. In particular, Angilee Wallises – Terry's mother – refused to believe that her son was "gone".... The Wallises made a bold decision. In spite of Terry's injury, they decided to incorporate him into traditional family activities as if nothing had ever happened.

Nineteen years went by. The Wallises acclimated to life with Terry. As unusual and demanding as his special needs were, they became just another part of the routine....

Almost exactly nineteen years to the day he'd been declared officially brain-dead – a miracle happened. Terry Wallis "woke up"....

His first words caught Angilee completely by surprise. Terry said, "Mom." Angilee nearly fainted. The next word he said was "Pam," the name of his longtime nurse. After that, Terry's vocabulary began to expand at an incredible rate. He was soon speaking in full sentences – joking, laughing, wondering what had happened.[19]

As seen in the Schiavo case, PVS is a troubling condition, not just for the psychology of family members, but for medicine itself. The case of another "Terry," Terry Wallis of Mountain View, Arkansas, showed a man who after nineteen years was said to have emerged from a permanent vegetative state – even, according to the website for his charitable fund, "brain-dead." Further investigation raised serious questions about his PVS diagnosis, indicating instead that he showed substantive signs of being "minimally conscious" (Fins 2005;

[19] From the "history" webpage of the Terry Wallis Fund (http://www.theterrywallisfund.org/history.html).

Wijdicks 2006). In recent years, many have turned to an additional category that resides between PVS and neuron clarity – the minimally conscious state (MCS). MCS was given a consensus-based diagnosis in 2002, and is characterized by "a condition of severely altered consciousness in which minimal, but definite, behavioral evidence of self or environmental awareness is demonstrated" (Giacino et al. 2002). MCS may have a number of causes, including congenital injuries, traumatic injuries, or progressive degeneration (Cranford 2002).

MCS became known to millions when Senator Bill Frist pro-nounced Terri Schiavo to be in a minimally conscious state after viewing a few seconds of a videotape with her and her mother. Autopsy later proved the claim of MCS to be wrong (her brain had atrophied too extensively), but questions about the consciousness of PVS patients persist, and the fMRI research begins to indicate that at least some patients diagnosed with PVS may have some cortical func-tions otherwise not indicated by their actions. In fact, some patients diagnosed in a VS have progressed to MCS, though there is contro-versy about whether this holds for "permanent" VS, since there is no verified evidence of such a transition taking place after more than twenty months in a vegetative state.[20]

At the same time, "some recent studies suggest that the diag-nostic distinction between MCS and PVS is missed by neurologists at rates that would be intolerable in other clinical domains" (Fins 2005). Of course this is troubling, as a diagnosis of PVS indicates permanent unconsciousness while MCS carries with it at least "min-imal" consciousness, and the possibility (even if currently unpre-dictable) of improvement (cf. Lammi et al. 2005).[21] However, the high rate of diagnostic error should not be surprising. Aside from

---

[20] Fins has rightly noted that getting better at diagnoses and prognoses matters, in part because we should want to be able to support both the right to die and the right to care – Terri Schiavo, on the one hand; Terry Wallis, on the other.

[21] Thus it is important to be clear that MCS is a condition in which patients show some improvement – from coma to VS to MCS. But this improvement can be hard to identify behaviorally, and we must be both vigilant and sensitive in our investigations – especially, though not exclusively, with patients who have had traumatic, not simply anoxic, brain injuries.

the fact that "a neurologist acting in good faith might examine an MCS patient when his level of arousal was low" (Fins 2005), consciousness is a complex philosophical, psychological, and medical issue. What are its constitutive elements? Are "hotspots" on a fMRI image enough? Must we be able to measure chemical changes? Does consciousness imply intentionality? Must intentionality be publicly identifiable through behavior? No deep consensus truly exists about these issues, though functional, practical consensus pushes us toward the idea that consciousness exists when personal awareness of one's environment exists.

So, if consciousness is even possible, and PVS is actually a form of severely diminished MCS, what then are the ethical implications? Having acknowledged that there is a typical concern for conscious individuals, this does not entail the moral claim that all consciousness is of equal value. Dogs, cats, pigs, and cows are all conscious in the everyday sense of that term, and yet for the most part we do not take them to have equal moral weight (whatever moral weight we give them, and some more than others) to normally functioning humans. On the other hand, persons with severe neurological compromise are not simply a-moral beings, beyond our concern.

It takes careful scrutiny to parse descriptions from desires, and in fact it can never be done entirely. However, situations like Ms. Schiavo's require that careful attention be paid to the way the interests of all parties are infusing themselves into the discussion. Whichever way one comes down, the right-to-life arguments are partially correct about one thing – it is Ms. Schiavo's life that is at stake, not ours. However, this does not finish the thought, for it is not just her life but her due respect – and life is empty without this – that is also at stake, and it obligates us to work even harder to protect not her *body* but her *dignity*. Of course that is precisely what both parties to the fray believed they were doing, and what that demonstrates is that the argument over Terri Schiavo's condition was more about who is best positioned to author the last chapter(s) of her life story, than it was about the medical "facts." In fact, the arguments about the medical condition were attempts to "be right" about her fate.

It would be hard for either party to disagree with the statement that tubes and machines can preserve a body, but only respectful consideration for her dignity would preserve her life. And yet all these wranglings and all these interventions diminished, not augmented, her life.

Thus, even here in the midst of a significant social controversy about a well-known case, we are reminded that narrative understandings of patients is often, at bottom, *the* moral issue. The issues here seem quite problematic, potentially conflicting, and ambiguous. Our diagnoses are imprecise, our learning still in flux. But what is involved with these concerns is not so much whether we can diagnosis with incontrovertible precision, but what are the implications for this patient's life as long as she resides in conditions of such significant neurological compromise?

A Note on Neurodegenerative Dementia

Straddling the space between "permanent" incapacitation and lucid-but-terminally-ill patients is a large group of individuals whose conditions, through various forms of progressive diseases, are "characterized by a general loss of intellectual abilities involving impairment of memory, judgment, and abstract thinking as well as changes in personality" (Dorland 1994, 439). While MCS patients have regained at least minimal consciousness, with the possibility that some of them may "emerge" out of MCS altogether, it is generally the case that when patients lose consciousness from a traumatic brain event, neurodegenerative disorders such as Alzheimer's, Huntington's chorea, multiple sclerosis, and Parkinson's slowly but progressively destroy brain tissue, eventually leaving the afflicted individual with no ability to control bodily movement or to contemplate intellectual problems. This eventual state may be MCS or something even more severe, where it is certainly (though cautiously) characterized as a permanent mental and physical incapacitation not wholly unlike that of someone in a PVS.

While I started off this chapter by suggesting that almost all patients discussed in the chapter are permanently confined to institutions, this was something of an exaggeration, for some of the neurologically demented remain for much (if not all) of their lives at home with family and friends. But even here, the percentage of those dying in institutions increases annually. And, the slow progression of many of these irreversible neurodegenerative diseases can provide time for the patient to attempt to cope with future conditions in a proactive way. Some develop formal advance directives; others simply make evolving plans with families and other caregivers. Unfortunately, too many patients do not adequately investigate the options, and make plans for the future, resulting in open-ended considerations being made by proxies once dementia has reduced these patients to a state of complete mental incapacitation, lacking even an awareness of self.

Decisions about Permanently Incapacitated Patients

For the most part, bioethicists were consistent in their conclusion that Ms. Schiavo's dying process should have been allowed to go forward without the intervention of artificial means of support – including nutrition and hydration. In part, this conclusion rested on the accepted idea that each person is autonomous and thus has the right to determine what can be done to her body. Of course, Ms. Schiavo's condition precluded her ability to speak on her own behalf, so coupled with the right of *self*-determination is the basic understanding that when patients are incapacitated, surrogates themselves are entitled to exercise this right on behalf of patients.

It would seem that decision making in all cases of the kinds of severely compromised patients discussed thus far must be done in light of the prognostic implications of the medical information available, and yet the level of diagnostic accuracy may be less important than the broad implications for the patient's life story.

Again, as we will recall, the radically empirical attitude is focused on lived experience, but experiences are not atomic; they come as part of a history, part of a community, part of a whole life-complex. Adults who have been neurologically devastated by injury or disease are individuals whose lives have been significantly altered, and it is reasonable to ask how these new conditions might best be understood in relation to the life lived previously. The trajectory and incorporation of the conditions of these kinds of patients we have discussed may well pose different kinds of specific answers to this question, and yet every one of these patients will be left to the decisions and actions of others. Here, then, we must turn to the use of advance directives and the practices of surrogate decision making.

I state again that the practical guide in medical decision making for the radically empirical attitude is to look toward the patient's narrative – her life story. While all persons are members of communities (familial, filial, and beyond), we have also discussed the importance of the patient's own *autho*ritative control of the story. No person writes her story alone, and yet deference to the individual whose story it is requires that we not attempt to create the narrative with our own inflections, unless we do so with a participatory, non-dictatorial, process.

Advance Directives

Deference to the patient herself is reflected in the acceptance of allowing the patient to create an advance directive (AD).[22] ADs have more than two decades of legal and moral standing (not without controversy), and they allow the patient (while still having decisional capacity) to express what she would or would not want if she were to be in a state of permanent incapacity. Some ADs specify treatment options to be accepted or avoided. Others identify individuals who are to act as proxies. Still others do both. The idea, then, is that ADs make it possible for the patient's voice to be heard even when she cannot speak; this recognizes that primary authorship resides with the patient – even at the end of life.[23]

And yet this is surely not the kind of authorship typically found in most life stories. In fact, life stories are metaphorical. We rarely write down our decisions for the day before we confront the day. Typically, our authoring is "on the fly," deciding and acting as we go. We might anticipate one environment or another significantly ahead of time (setting up for a holiday party weeks in advance; scheduling surgery around a work schedule), but most of life's narrative occurs

---

[22] In this section, the focus on ADs is a focus primarily on "living wills." The following section on "surrogate decision making" covers the points to be made about the function of a healthcare proxy or someone holding a durable power of attorney for healthcare for another.

[23] For a comprehensive account of many legal and moral issues surrounding ADs, see King 1996 and an earlier collection of essays edited by Hackler, Moseley, and Vawter (1989).

in media res. ADs, thus, while attempting to extend our voices and provide control, do so in an artificial way.[24] This poses at least two practical problems for ADs.

First, most ADs are vague, general, and conditional. They must be applied under difficult and unique situations, and yet are written with little experience of these kinds of situations in mind. They often speak about retaining, withholding, or withdrawing life-sustaining treatments, but just what constitutes those kinds of treatments can be complicated. If blood pressure is falling, should pressors be used? If the patient is already on a mechanical ventilator, should CPR be performed? If she is not on a vent, and an infection compromises the lungs, should a vent be used temporarily; should antibiotics? Typically, this level of detailed decision making is not written into an AD, and if it were, the AD could become difficult and cumbersome to apply in an emergency.

To some degree the issue of specificity and clarity cannot be overcome. Detailed decision making takes an understanding of operative details, and all of them cannot be known ahead of time. However, several programs exist to help develop meaningful and useful ADs, some focusing on the values of the patient (e.g., "Five Wishes"), others focusing on clarifying physician orders (e.g., POLST – Physician Orders for Life-Sustaining Treatment). Putting ADs into a broader perspective, though, can remind us that these documents are ways of authoring elements of our end-of-life story. And like the sketch of a book chapter, the details need not always be present for the information to be significant. It can be useful, therefore, to create a document (or documents) that not only explains *what* medical interventions are or are not desired, but *why* they are. This can help decision makers and caregivers place one's expressed *means* of care into a more richly understood view of the ends one wishes to achieve – be that peace, harmony, dignity, self-determination.

Second, what do most of us know about the conditions we might face? PVS and MCS are conditions we cannot know about ahead of time. The decline into dementia can in fact look to others as if it is a

---

[24] This is what Rebecca Dresser call "an incomplete form of self-determination" (1989) and what leads Allen Buchanan (1987) to claim that ADs lack moral force since they lack contemporaneous decision making.

happy, contented state. Does the shift to these new conditions in our lives even call into question whether we are the same self we were before? Can ADs function effectively if we are in fact not the people we thought we would be in these conditions? These questions have been debated in the literature for many years,[25] and the radically empirical take on experience allows for selves to adapt and change, making these kinds of questions especially poignant.

However, for the radical shift of conditions that is characterized by permanent incapacity, there seems to be no way to account for a sense of new "self" for such individuals. If, as I have argued throughout, a radically empirical attitude warrants a narrative view of patients and their participation in the authoring of their stories, then especially for those who literally cannot speak for themselves, ADs provide a basis for helping author the stories according to their values and interest as they can best be understood (cf. Rich 1997). This, too, argues for more richly presented ADs, with both the *what* and *why* spelled out.

For all of medicine's newly emphasized concern for pain and suffering, some patients will find indignity a much greater burden. For them, ADs provide the opportunity to avoid *what to them* would be an undignified existence. In a world of plural values, no reasonable argument can be made that their sense of indignity at the prospect of permanent decisional incapacity is unacceptable. Such a position speaks to people's own life stories, and need not express any morally negative response about those who do continue to live under such conditions.

With those who have diminishing capacity through longer onset processes, it should be clear from the previous discussions that the morally appropriate act is to make them participants in their care to the extent possible, "triangulating" gaps in the story with written documents, such as ADs, as well as knowledge of their current life

---

[25] There is a rich literature on the status of ADs for demented patients (see Dresser 1989, 1995; Kadish 1992; Dworkin 1993; Callahan 1995; Newton 1999; Groves 2006). There are important questions of "selfhood" and the applicability of ADs if dementia significantly changes a person's sense of self and ways of experiencing life. These concerns are particularly applicable to those whose degenerative process is slow and wavering, not resulting in complete incapacity or unconsciousness.

experiences and previously understood values and interests. In other words, no single answer can be given, save for one that champions a process of inclusion through conversation, documentation, and imagination.[26] These same practices apply to all surrogate decision making when no clear ADs exist, and so we turn to those cases now.

Surrogate Decision Making

When no clear statement is available from the patient about future treatment, someone else must make health care decisions for her. That "someone" may be identified through such legal documents as "healthcare proxies" or durable powers of attorney for healthcare, or they may be identified according to legal statutes that typically identify next-of-kin decision makers. Either way, the person identified is charged to act as a true "surrogate," where *surrogate* decision making for adult patients has traditionally been described as a process that should strive to extend respect for *patient* autonomy. Difficulties arise, however, since the surrogate is left to her own devices in order to decide on future medical treatment. Given that these decisions are always *about* some patient and never directly *with* that patient, the proxy is called upon to attempt to make decisions from the "point of view" of the patient. This is often called applying the principle of "substituted judgment," where decisions by surrogates should be made by taking into account what can reasonably be determined to be what the patient herself would have decided if she were able. That is, the surrogate should use the patient's expressed interests and behaviors to indicate what should be done. Taking on the patient's view is an imaginative projection of the patient's known interests, prior to incapacity, into the current debilitating circumstances; it takes a great deal of sensitivity and moral artistry. These situations place the proxy in the position of sympathizer and empathizer, demanding that she speak as the patient would speak if she were still able. To put it in narrative terms, the surrogate attempts to author the final chapter of the patient's story using (as best as possible) the patient's

---

[26] The research of Teno and colleagues (2007) demonstrates that the process of developing advance directives, while far from perfect, can have positive outcomes for patient care and family comfort with decision making.

narrative voice (cf. Churchill J. 1989; Blustein 1999; Kuczewski 1999; Torke et at. 2008).

Of course, this task is best handled by someone who knows the patient's values and interests intimately. Even then, there are no guarantees that the proxy and patient will speak with the *same* voice on these matters. The extent to which the patient was close to the surrogate is the extent to which the surrogate will be able to make decisions that the patient might have, for it is through intimate connections that the truth about ourselves is revealed to others. As James puts it, we "respond to the truth in [each other] by taking [each other] truly and seriously, too" (James [1899a], 646).

Given the usual closeness of familial bonds, relatives are often appointed to this surrogate role, though a broad base of family and friends may be useful for the task of finding the "true" voice of the patient (see Burt 2005, S12–13). However, the very fact that we are individuals distinctly engaged with our own perspectives means that there will always be some gap between what others are and what we take others to be, regardless of the degree of intimacy we have with them. Couple this gap with the fact that little is ever discussed about end-of-life issues, even between intimate family members, and it should be no surprise that the SUPPORT (1995) study found that surrogate decision makers did only better than chance at understanding what the patient would actually want for end-of-life care.[27]

So if the proxy does *not* attempt to "put on the shoes" of the patient, then it would seem the proxy decides based primarily on her interests or those of the healthcare professionals who are providing options. The proxy thus fails to capture the patient's perspective, attaching herself to some other guiding principle, and therefore may follow a process that is intended mainly to meet the interests of others. To the extent that we accept that the self is a social product and should be allowed, when fully capable, to be an active narrator of her own story within society, however, this approach by a proxy to an incapacitated patient seems by extension unwarranted. It takes

---

[27] The SUPPORT study is oft-cited landmark research, but many have noted problems – be they factual, psychological, ethical, or practical – with surrogate decision making. A review of many of these issues can be found in Berger et al. 2008.

away the voice of the person for whom these activities are to be performed, and once again we will end up losing sight of the "right healing action" for the particular patient.

Conclusion

The ambiguity inherent in trying to adopt the values and interest of another creates a clear and troubling possibility for conflict. On the one hand, there are struggles among family members or other decision makers about the best way to conclude the patient's life story. On the other hand, there are conflicts between proxies and medical personnel.

The former was illustrated clearly in the division over Terri Schiavo's care, with her husband claiming that Ms. Schaivo wanted to be allowed to die without the use of medical technologies, and her parents claiming that her Catholic faith would have led her to want assisted nutrition and hydration. This is a challenge for decision makers and caregivers alike. Nothing gives clear *a priori* priority to one narrative account over the other save for cultural conventions concerning the nature of the relationship between married persons and the relationship of daughters to parents. Legally, most state laws give priority to the spouse as the decision maker over parents, but this legal fact does not always capture the felt experiences of closeness or distance between relatives. Of course, the law then allows the circumvention of this traditional prioritiy of marriage by providing the option of naming a healthcare proxy specifically. However, few people do so. Does this mean that all married persons who do not provide this kind of AD want their spouses to make decisions? Surely not, and yet how are healthcare providers to know whom to listen to?

Frankly, the legal mechanisms are probably best as policy, and yet there is a moral answer to these questions – namely, a thorough investigation of the patient's life story from as many parties as possible in order to provide the groundwork for authoring the last chapter. For example, in the Schiavo case, Ms. Schiavo's 2004 court-appointed Guardian Ad Litem, John Wolfson, determined that there was evidence in support of Michael Schiavo's claim that his wife wanted to avoid technological prolongment, with no countervailing evidence.

This may not satisfy because the stories are inexact, and authorship is not a scientific endeavor. Ambiguity will remain, and that fact may always carry some discomfort with it.

Conflicts between proxies and medical personnel often arise from ambiguities and lack of clarity. This is not to say that some conflicts do not come down to specific intractable differences, but many occur because we fail to understand how the means of care fit with the goals of care – that is, we fail to match our medical practices, technologies, obligations, and concerns to reasonable ends to be achieved for a particular patient's life story. And this occurs because we, both families and physicians, fail to understand clearly the situation (medically, culturally, and personally) and its implications (medically, culturally, and personally). On the one hand, families, captured by grief and a desire to protect their loved one's interests do not always hear the diagnosis and prognosis; they do not always grasp the realities of the medical condition. On the other hand, physicians, focused on treatment, expertise, and futility, often forget to listen to families or, more commonly, speculate about what families want based on what families do and say. Families often don't know how to express their desires, nor do they have the experience and knowledge to express more than a limited number of desires and the means to achieve them. It is rare for both parties to have a clear and frank discussion about goals of care – what is desirable and what is achievable and why. Why for many patients with severe neurological compromise do physicians and nurses think that more medicine is either futile or harmful? Why in the face of such conditions do families think more medicine is helpful and beneficial? Don't both parties want what is best for the patient?

In order to explore these issues more fully, in order to create a space that can find common ground at a deeper level, a conversation that gets at the heart of what is truly desired and reasonably achievable must take place. The conversation is meant to elicit information, to be a cooperative inquiry into the issues that arise in the situation. As such, it should follow a few useful insights about cooperative inquiry, such as James's own recognition that the whole of truth is not available to any one person. Therefore one should not act as if she is immune from criticism, and in turn admit her lack of knowledge when she is, in fact, ignorant on a particular point. These guidelines (and others, e.g., Hook 2002, 294–295) shape our moral attitudes toward the rules of inquiry, but the content is best focused on what the goals of care are. This fact seems such a truism as to be trivial, and yet we are not terribly good at eliciting both the goals and the reasons for them from patients and families. Instead, we speculate and extrapolate from the few cues we do get – family comments, body language, personal projection.

Physician must ask families directly and without speculation:

- What are the family's goals of care? What is its vision of the future for their loved one. What are they hoping for? What do they fear?
  - Why do they hold the goals they do?

And physicians must clarify for themselves:

- What facts/information are provided by the family in support of those goals (or that vision)?
  - What is the family's understanding of the situation at hand?
- What values and interests do they express in support of those goals (or that vision)?
  - What is the life story they tell that brings them here and reaches into the future?

Physicians should continue by putting these goals and clarifications in context:

- Given the family's expressed interests and goals, what means (if any) are available and appropriate? Can we achieve what they are hoping for?
  - Are there significant barriers to achieving the goals? If we can't achieve them, why not?
    - Do those barriers arise from a conflict with the law
    - commonly accepted moral norms
    - cultural differences
    - psychological/cognitive factors
    - your personal values
    - your professional obligations
    - your skills and abilities

- available resources or finances
- the limits of current medical science and technology
- other
- Of the conflicts identified, are any intractable?
  - If yes, why?
  - If no, what means are appropriate to overcoming them?

If necessary, then, physicians must ask themselves:

- Are there more reasonable goals for the patient/family (that is, should their goals be redirected)? What hopes *can* we achieve or should we try to achieve?
  - *Why* are these goals more reasonable given what you have learned about the condition and prognosis of the patient and the interests and goals of the patient/family?
  - What are the appropriate means to achieving these "more reasonable" goals?

This line of investigation cannot guarantee that conflicts will be resolved,[28] and other possibilities for conflict resolution in end-of-life decision making exist (see Dubler 2005). However, what should be noted is that this kind of discussion about goals of care places the emphasis on the importance of cooperative achievement in developing the patient's final storyline.[29] Since the patient cannot exercise any self-determination, we *must* rely on the careful, sensitive efforts

---

[28] A discussion of "goals" may be too devoid of emotive qualities to capture a more robust expression of familial/patient experiences. Thus, as shown in the parenthetical remark, reframing these concepts in terms of the more affective concepts of "hope" *and* "fears" (we are driven as much by avoidance as aspiration) may be more successful at opening up conversation by engaging not in dispassionate reasoning but in emotive considerations as well. I want to be clear that I do not take the concepts, "goals" and "hopes/fears," to be synonymous. They are intimately related and differ mainly (and importantly!) in their emotive contents and scope (see Feudtner 2007 and Shade 2001). Frankly, though, a focus on goals of care is best handled *before* conflict arises, as part of the development of good care-planning for the patient.

[29] Again, I turn to Fins (2006), who has developed an insightful analysis and helpful guide to ways to approach "goals of care" at the end of life. While I hope that my questions prove a useful start, Fins's account is more comprehensive and robust, placing the discussion in the context of what he calls a "palliative ethic of care." Along with his discussion, Fins offers the Goals of Care Assessment Tool (GCAT),

of the proxy decision maker(s) to help determine the action that best fits the patient's known interests, values, and obligations in light of the best medical evidence provided by careful, sensitive medical personnel. As long as proxies attempt to make a decision from the patient's point of view – tolerating and overcoming the appreciable differences in their interests – the proxy decision-making process (a process done not in isolation, but in cooperation) attempts to substitute itself as precisely as possible for an imagined self-determining process by the patient herself.[30] Thus, the proxy decision making mirrors the process of the patient as if she were of sound decision-making capacity even though terminally ill. Of course, as we have already discussed in previous chapters, the patient's desires do not settle the issue by themselves, but they do help locate and focus the decision making since the patient will be someone directly affected by what decisions are made. Countervailing interests may prevail, no doubt, but they must do so, as far as possible, in light of the interest of the patient herself, and preferably not in ignorance of them.

developed several years earlier in conjunction with colleagues (Fins et al. 1999), as a "preventative" ethical instrument.

[30] Recall James's discussion of overcoming human blindness by tolerating and even appreciating the differences between individuals and the values they hold (see my Chapter 2).

6

Dying Young

What Interests Do Children Have?

> Why isn't it easier when a child dies?
> Their lives so short, unencumbered and free.
> But then again, we all may indeed suffer so.
> The uncertainty of every child's fate lies
> With people who may love and care but cannot see
> How little – and how much – they actually know.
>
> *(for Caroline) D.M. Hester*

Our radically empirical attitude toward dying has led us through a survey of issues raised by different groups of adult patients. Since we are to take all and only experience, as a practical matter this means approaching patients as robust narratives, engaging their life stories and the complex interrelations to others and environment that those stories express and entail. For the most part, I have argued that this approach, while remaining contextual and social in scope and interpretation, still must promote the participation of individual patients, and attempt to champion the stories they wish to tell. While patients' stories, as expressed by them through their own voices or written directives, should not be taken as *necessarily* determinative, they have authorial force.

I will now turn to pediatric patients prematurely facing death – specifically to issues concerning neonatal end-of-life care. Here the presumption of patients' "authority" in their own narratives gives way to others, as these patients are still greatly underdeveloped. But then what would it mean to implement the radically empirical insights so far discussed? In infancy, much of a child's life story is being written, if not by her, then by others (parents, physicians, and so forth), and careful analysis of the interests expressed about such a patient becomes worthy of pursuit.

As with the discussion of adult patients, there is no way to do justice to all the different kinds of pediatric patients who face the end of life all too soon, not to mention doing justice to individual cases themselves. I will, thus (as noted already) restrict my discussion to infant patients in pediatric care (recognizing that this does a disservice to many others) – in particular, severely impaired neonates and the concept of "best interests" for determining care.

What We Mean by Neonatal "Interests"[1]

At birth, Grace Johnson had a lower than normal heart rate, was making no effort to breathe, and exhibited no movement of her extremities. She was quickly incubated and supported by a mechanical ventilator. Diagnostic testing revealed that she had experienced a hemorrhage high in the cervical spinal cord.

Over the next week, the Johnsons' neonatologist consulted the literature and searched internationally for experts with experience in treating the type of spinal cord injury suffered by Baby Grace. According to a physician who had dealt with approximately twenty such birth injuries, decisions had been made to terminate or not to institute ventilator support at the time of or soon after birth in about 50 percent of cases. Approximately 25 percent of the babies that were ventilator supported died before one year of age. The prognosis for breathing without a ventilator and for moving extremities would probably be apparent by about six weeks after birth.

Mr. and Mrs. Johnson were clear from the outset that they believed a life of total paralysis and ventilator dependence was not in Grace's best interest. However, they wished to wait and give Grace a chance to demonstrate her potential for recovery before deciding to withdraw ventilator support. The team agreed that the choice should rest with the parents and that withdrawing ventilator support was ethically permissible.

---

[1] The following section is adapted from Hester 2007.

Over the next eleven weeks, Grace's mother was at her bedside for most of every day, and her father visited every evening and on weekends. They held and nurtured Grace and participated in her routine baby care, but declined to learn suctioning or ventilator management because they were determined that she would not live her life on a ventilator. There were glimmers of hope – occasional movement of one side of the diaphragm, some random movements of the extremities. She responded to her environment and caregivers with facial expressions, and there were no indications that she would experience significant cognitive impairment. But attempts to wean the ventilator support were unsuccessful, and it became clear that there was little if any recovery in the spinal cord.

Grace's parents consulted the same experts contacted by the neonatologist, requested a second opinion about her prognosis, and did a lot of research. They sought input from family members and spoke with two priests. They contacted the National Spinal Cord Association and received information from hospital staff about services and financial assistance available both short and long term. They felt that the outlook was grim for Grace's quality of life despite the best that technology had to offer. They could cite statistics about the impact of such serious medical conditions on marriages, careers, and any future children. They spoke eloquently of a child who would be unable to play sports, couldn't draw pictures for the refrigerator door, would live in fear of the ventilator becoming disconnected, would experience many hospitalizations, could die from any routine respiratory virus, and would know what she was missing because she had normal cognitive function.

At three months, the parents requested discontinuation of the ventilator, knowing this would result almost immediately in Grace's death. The family decided against adoption because their concern was not her impact on them, but her own best interest.

While they had some staunch advocates within the health care team, the neonatologist and some others felt strongly that withdrawal of support was no longer an option. Grace's medical condition was stable, and she had become a person to them. They suggested that in a few years she might be a candidate for a diaphragmatic pacemaker and might then be ventilator-dependent only when sleeping. With braces and a standing table, she might one day stand, and with computers she could operate a wheelchair and other equipment. Everyone knew of someone as impaired as Grace who seemed to have led a fairly complete and happy life and had even managed to excel in something. (McAiley and Daley 2002, 12)

While this is well-trodden territory in the ethics literature, I focus on severely impaired neonates because at first blush it looks as though making decisions about their care raises the same moral issues as making decisions for incapacitated adults. Like cognitively and communicatively compromised adults, children often, and neonates always, lack the ability to express clearly their experiences to us. Crying, while probably more than just a reflexive action, always requires significant interpretation by others, and much of that interpretation is based on the consequences to the crying child when certain actions are performed. If she stops crying when given food, we say that the crying *meant* she was hungry. Legitimacy of any imposition of intentionality of expression remains an unsettled issue. For the severely impaired and compromised newborn child, the question concerning what, if anything, she experiences, and what, if any, intentional interests she has is seemingly impossible to answer.

Thus the similarity between newborns and incapacitated adults quickly breaks down because while with adults we can typically attempt to extrapolate from their previous actions, stated interests and values, and any shared experiences to fashion an idea of what might be appropriate medical care, no such basis is available to us with infants. In fact, the force of the concern for "expressed" interests is felt acutely with neonates in a peculiar way: We are left solely to our own experiences to make decisions about them. Taking their experiences seriously, then, always amounts to our attributing something not from their previously enacted, reflective self to their current conditions (as attempted with surrogate decision making for adults). We should always be sensitive when dealing with persons who may be experiencing the world in positive, significant ways that we cannot recognize; however, we will never know exactly what neonatal experiences are, or even whether neonates can be said to be cognitively aware of any of their experiences.

In the language of bioethics, then, we are without recourse to "substituted judgment" for newborns. More significant relative to the arguments throughout this book, infants are not the authors of their own life stories – at least, not in an identifiable way. That is, we cannot be said to be making decisions that mirror those they themselves would make if they could. What, then, is our recourse in decision making? Traditionally, bioethics under such conditions leads us to use "best interests" to make medical determinations (cf.

President's Commission 1983). It is frequent in the literature, and more importantly at the bedside, to be confronted with the idea that the task of caregivers and neonatal decision makers is to do what is in the best interest of the child.[2] While it is not without meaning for us to ask what is in the best interest of adult patients who lack decisional capacity, for most of these adult patients we extrapolate from what we do know (if anything) about them as decision makers and persons who express interests. What follows is that the less we know about their interests, the more we are left to wonder whose or what interests should prevail, and why.

Unlike the adult setting, this circumstance of the "unknown" is *de facto* the case for neonates since the patient is not able to express (and has never expressed) her interests. Thus, whatever "best interests" is supposed to amount to must be imported from sources other than the individual patient. To paraphrase Tristram Engelhardt (1975; 1987), our decisions are always about them and never with them.[3] And as John Lantos correctly notes, "All we can do is try to reason by analogy, try to extrapolate somehow from our own experiences and perspectives or perhaps to incorporate the responses of some other more articulate group. But which group?" (2001, 40–41)

Left only with "other" resources or groups, how can we evaluate and weigh the importance of the many sources from which interests come? Though many have asked this question concerning "best interests," and some have even applied this concern within the context of neonatal decision making, what is offered here is a kind of "taxonomy" of the multiple sources that vie for attention during

---

[2] It is important to note, along with Loretta Kopelman, that there is another set of decision-making guidelines for neonates, the so-called Baby Doe regulations. However, while they are still part of the legal landscape, I accept Kopelman's (2005) comprehensive refutation of their moral authority.

[3] In his careful analysis of the President's Commission (1983) and Baby Doe regulations (1984), John Arras (1984) attempts to analyze "what should be done" for children from "who should decide." His analysis is helpful for gaining some perspective and conceptual clarity, but it should be clear in light of the preceding insights that determining "what to do" is necessarily intertwined with "who decides." That is, the interests that are at play arise from someone's perspective, and weighing not just the claims made but the relationship of that someone to the infant under consideration is all part of what it means to come to a reasonable moral decision.

"best interest" determinations about neonates (for any patient, in point of fact). It is my concern that in clinical settings we typically narrow the scope of interest-sources for neonates too quickly, and thus focus too pointedly on just two sources of interests: avoiding harm, and parents. While there are good reasons for both focuses, neither alone is morally acceptable, and as a more comprehensive awareness of possible interest-sources will demonstrate, they ignore a great many other real sources of interest. If "best interests" is to guide us, we should be clear on what interests take precedence, and why. So it should help us to identify those sources – at least in broad ways.

It should be recognized that most clinicians, consultants, and families would recognize many of these interest-sources once pointed out, though few are ever given serious consideration in lieu of the current centrality of the legalistic threshold of negligence or abuse (harm) on the one hand, and parental interests (often described in terms of rights) on the other. In light of this narrow focus of interests in much of our considered medical deliberations, what would it mean to take the broader range of interests seriously in our moral considerations? I suggest that a narrative approach to decision making, as well as a focus on goals of care, is robust enough to do the job. This approach and emphasis do not undo either parental decision making or avoiding harm as primary concerns, but they better situate the traditional primacy of parents and "do no harm" for moral deliberation in order to avoid reduction and exclusion of the complexity of interest-sources pressing on newborn medical decision making.

There are several models of decision making for children, and I begin with what might be called a "traditional" account of the "best interest" standard. The account begins with what Allen Buchanan and Dan Brock (B&B) have called the value of "the protection and promotion of [the child's] well-being" (1989, 227), with "best interest" defined as decisions that look at the individual child's well-being – that is, decisions that are "self-regarding." By emphasizing that, where possible, children should be participants in their healthcare decision, this traditional view attempts to support the importance of self-determination. However, in so doing, B&B are careful to note the obvious fact that children are not always capable of good self-determined decisions. So what are we left with when a child does not demonstrate decisional capacity (and surely neonates are without decisional capacity)? B&B explain that along with well-being and self-determination, a third value exists – parental decision making. Following the legal tradition, B&B claim that parents are the appropriate decision makers for their children, but parental decisions should always be made in accord with a child's best interest. When focused on infants, this line of reasoning can lead to a difficult circle, and what they say poses little help in avoiding circularity. For example, B&B emphasize that "the question the decision making is supposed to be answering is *not* what would be best for *[the decision maker]*, but what would be best for the *infant*" (252). However, when making decisions for infants (and in particular, those with severe impairments), they employ a "reasonable person" standard that relies on what a "rational (or reasonable) person [would] prefer," and specifically whether such a person would prefer "to terminate such a life in order to end its pain and suffering" (253). The reasonable person standard, though, does not directly answer the "question decision making is supposed to be answering," since, according to B&B's own standard, there is no necessary logical or practical relationship between what a determination of what an abstract "reasonable person" would want and what is in the "interest" of the infant herself – unless, of course, B&B believe that all infants are alike.[4] If so, then it is not clear what the significant force of their requirement that it be in the *infant's* interest amounts to. That is, either more information must be given as to what a reasonable person is to consider as relevant to any specific *infant's* interests, or B&B have not provided an acceptable substitute for their own "*self*-regarding" condition for "best interests."

On the other hand, Lainie Friedman Ross in her book *Children, Families, and Health Care Decision Making* (1998), supports B&B's valuing of parental decision making, but argues against what she calls their narrow conception of "best interest." Since B&B equate "best

---

4 There are several critiques of the use of the "reasonable person" standard for making decisions about "imperiled newborns." See, for example, Robertson 1975 and Arras 1984, though there are many others.

interests" with "self-regarding" determinations, Ross correctly notes that their view is highly individualistic. Such a "narrow" view puts restraints on parents as decision makers, specifically questioning whether "familial objectives" can be appropriate in "best interest" determinations for a child. That is, parents, employing the "reasonable person" standard, are confined by B&B's account to focus "best interests" on an insular sense of patient interests. Instead, Ross argues for a "constrained parental autonomy" that requires parents on the one hand (at a "minimum," we might say), to provide for the "basic needs" of the child," and on the other hand (as a goal) to respect the child as a person – that is, to promote long-term (or lifetime) autonomy.[5] And these requirements are identified in order to identify the range of allowable parental decisions. Understood in this way, Ross argues that her "constrained parental autonomy" takes seriously "intrafamilial trade-offs . . . provided that each child's basic needs are procured" (51). "Familial interests," then, are not to be ignored when making decisions about a child's care. Describing a form of "intimate group" (described as "a group in which members derive benefit if not identity from membership . . . in which members try to accommodate one another's needs rather than disengage" [34]),[6] Ross's account opens up decision making beyond simply "self-regarding" interests in order to take seriously the fact that children are intimately related and affected by their families and their familial situations. Thus, Ross's position changes the perspective on pediatric decision making.

There is no doubt that B&B rightly capture the moral fact that parents are in a unique, privileged position vis-à-vis their children

---

[5] The latter constraint is not to be understood narrowly as respecting the child as "competent" [sic. – i.e., with decisional capacity]. Children may make reasonable decisions that are, however, only informed by "limited experience, so that their decisions are not part of a well-conceived life plan" (61). As such, Ross supports parental authority (duly constrained as she suggests) in decision making "even after the child has developed some threshold level of competence" (66).

[6] In Ross's account of "intimate groups," the reader will probably recognize the similarities with the account of "community" given in Chapter 2. Here, Ross might disagree that "community" is the correct model for families – see her distinction between *Gemeinschaft* (translated: "community") and *Gesellschaft* (translated: "organization") (1998 28–34), but this may be more a difference of the terms that we have employed rather than the conceptual function they perform.

when it comes to decision making for their children. Further, as has already been noted, in the case of neonates, no ability to fall back on such concepts as "substituted judgment" is available to us. Thus, some other decision-making standard has to be applied. B&B's suggestion of "best interests" seems to meet with common sense, and yet Ross rightly analyzes their logic to show that they have far too narrow a definition of "best interest" for it to be useful. Further, Ross's own recognition that the familial environment must be considered in decision making for children nicely opens up the idea of "interests" to more than those that are "self-regarding."

It is perhaps only trivial to note that both B&B and Ross embed (different) reflexive concepts into their accounts, and both accounts are problematic. On the one hand, B&B's concept of "self-regard" is almost nonsensical when applied to children (and especially newborns) given that it is lack of "self" (see Chapter 2) that characterizes the newborn state, and is the source of frustration in decision making in the first place. On the other hand, Ross's concept of "constrained parental autonomy" seems oddly termed given that "autonomy" is classically defined as "self-determination," and yet what is at issue here is determining care for someone else, the newborn patient.[7] That is, these cases should be taken as paradigmatic of non-pejorative paternalism (or *parentalism*) rather than as "autonomous." It is because these decisions concern others that concern for what might be the limits on such decision making is so pronounced.

It is here at the "limits" of parental decision making that Doug Diekema (2004) has argued that as a practical and legalistic matter, our *modus operandi* has not been some form of the "best interest" standard, but instead a concern to follow the "harm principle." That is, on the one hand, medical professionalism is under an ethic of

---

7   In fairness, Ross may object to my critique of the use of the term "parental autonomy" because she believes that "children are incompetent and should not have health care autonomy" (1998, 66). As such, she may take parental decision making about their own children to be "autonomous" insofar as the parents are entitled to impose their own values on children, constrained by the requirement that they provide for the "basic needs" and promote the "long-term" autonomy of the child. Also, it may be helpful to note that Ross is not the only one to use "autonomy" in regards to parental decision-making – cf. Miller 2003.

"do no harm," and on the other hand, the law typically only delimits parental decision-making rights when parental decisions prove to be legally negligent or abusive. Specifically, then, "the harm principle provides a basis for identifying the threshold for state action" (250). Diekema's position addresses only the minimalist constraint of Ross's account in that he champions a view of pediatric decision making that does not aim specifically at some goal to achieve, but instead is constrained by some defined limit. However, while Ross's "lower" threshold is only one half of her account,[8] this negative limit for Diekema is his operating principle. Further, Ross is focused primarily on the *moral* argument concerning parental constraints, while Diekema's principle establishes the point at which the state is "justified in interfering with parental decisions regarding the health care of children" (250). In order to distinguish decisions that meet this "harm" threshold, Diekema lists several questions, the answers to which help determine whether a decision is or is not beyond the limits of the harm principle (see Diekema 2005, 252). His claim is that the reality of practical decision making demonstrates that "parents cannot and should not always be expected to make decisions that are in the child's best interest" (258) and that the "harm principle" sufficiently pinpoints whether the parents (when their decisions are not harmful) or the state (when parental decisions are harmful) should take over decision making.[9]

---

[8] While Ross understands "basic needs" as only half the story, Richard Miller, starting from liberal political theory (like Rawls), has singularly emphasized "basic interests" (aka "primary goods") as the grounding for parental determinations, since as a liberal he prefers to avoid any robust theory of the good that would be imposed upon moral agents. His account of "primary goods," then, is decidedly developed to define "basic interests" in such a way that it "provides a reasonable pluralism that allows for goods other than autonomy" (2003, 133). Much more can be said about Miller's account, but focused selectivity on my account requires me to leave any discussion aside.

[9] To be clear, Diekema specifically qualifies his use of the harm principle as applying in cases of parental refusal of treatment and only for the consideration of state intervention. That is, Diekema's discussion, while consciously set in the context of "best interests," is not intended to apply in all situations where the issue of "best interests" arises such as controversies raised by parental *demands* for treatment – for example, demand for dialysis as kidneys shut down in an infant with severe congenital cardiac anomalies. So, again, Diekema does not explain what would guide treatment decisions, but only what would limit parental refusals.

However, even if Diekema's position is descriptively correct, it is not clear that it should hold as morally normative. Here, an analogy concerning the limits of following the principle of respect for autonomy may be helpful. Respect for autonomy requires that individuals be given the ability to make self-determined decisions in absence of constraints; Beauchamp and Childress even claim that as a paradigm in healthcare, autonomy amounts to "*express* and informed consent" (1996, 121).[10] As I have argued elsewhere (Hester 2001), while this is a necessary component of ethically acceptable medical relationships, it is not sufficient. Such a negative moral requirement is not enough. Instead, a positive requirement of promoting participation is what should ground morally acceptable patient–professional relationships. Likewise, avoiding harm to children is itself morally necessary, but not ultimately sufficient. Something more positive must be provided as the moral ground of decision making for children.

It may now behoove us to return to a positive conception of "best interests," remembering that, on the one hand, best interests narrowly conceived do not adequately address the complex realities of neonatal life, and on the other, ideally conceived they may simply be beyond what is possible in practice. That is, both narrow interest considerations and an idealized concept of what is "best" fail to capture the textures of lived experience.[11] In light of these issues, Loretta Kopelman, in recent work on the subject (2005), has clarified a position that eschews "idealizing" best interests in order to strive for something that is practical and, as she has said elsewhere, "good enough." Her account, it would seem, attempts a more positive presumption for interest determinations than the use of either "avoiding harm" or "providing basic needs," but it remains carefully circumscribed. Kopelman's view does not focus on weighting

---

[10] This quote is from the 4th edition of Beauchamp and Childress, *The Principles of Biomedical Ethics*. In the 5th edition (2001, 65), the sentence drops the word "informed," but no reason is given for this change to the text and the claim.

[11] Brian Carter and Steven Leuthner (2002) have made similar arguments as Kopelman and, following economist Herbert Simon, have called such decisions as not "best" or "ideal," but "satisficing." As Carter and Leuthner say, "When dealing with hard choices, satisficing allows one to consider decisions that, while not perfect and not leaving one completely satisfied, satify to some extent and "suffice," given the constraints made on the decision-making process" (14).

considerations toward any one set of interests or a particular interest group, but instead attempts to delineate better the aims of such decisions. She notes three aspects of the "Best Interest Standard" that are operative in "best interest" claims – best interests as threshold, best interests as ideal, and best interests as demonstrating reasonableness (1997). First, "best interests" means not abusing or neglecting children. Second, "best interests" means recognizing our duties to promote the good of children. Third, "best interests" means doing what is reasonable given the conditions. Each of these three meanings has a role in best interest determination, but the first only sets the negative limits below which we may not go, and this does not help us determine what, among the range of positive possibilities, we may do. The second meaning, Kopelman recognizes, may be misconstrued with a more traditional "idealized" view of "best interests," which she believes is untenable. As she says, "It would not be possible for the Best Interest Standard to provide practical guidance for decision makers if it required what was ideal for the incompetent person" (2005, 349). In sum, these two meanings of "best interest" become arguments for recognizing specific "duties to the incompetent [sic.] individual" and reasonable "consensus about what choices are unacceptable" (2005, 349). The duties themselves are minimal, and the limits on acceptable choice place an emphasis on a "negative" standard. However, she still has a third possible meaning of "best interests," which, though related to the others (as she suggests), I would argue is the more important and often more practical one, whenever we attempt to do as much as the conditions merit, taking account of our abilities, authority, and limits.

What Kopelman calls "idealizing" *is* untenable, but I would argue that this is the case because people have not developed a sufficiently pragmatic view of ideals. In particular, those who argue that "best interests" push too far in the direction of championing the "ideal" over the "practical" (as if these two are a strict dichotomy) suffer from accepting a poor conceptual analysis of "ideals" that places them outside lived experience. Kopelman herself seems unable to avoid implying that this "ideal" character of the "Best Interest Standard" is operative when she states that "best interest" cannot "require people to do what is ideal" (349). That is, her own account seems to accept idealists' desires as correct in principle, but not in practice. But if we take Kopelman at her word, her own view of the matter may sound "defeatist" – that is, since we cannot reach "true" best interest, we are left to approximate fairly good interests. But why sound deflated – concerned that ideals in their "true" sense are always beyond our grasp, left otherwise with what is just "good enough"?

The problem here is that in many accounts, "ideal" and "best" begin from beyond the practical realities and finite and limited characteristics of the world. Instead, if we begin with the *radically* empirical insight that "ideals," whatever else they are, are part of lived experience, not outside it, and "best" interests are not strictly set off from practical matters, but are only meaningful when practically conceived. This, we recall is precisely the point James makes about ideals (see the discussion in Chapter 3), tying their significance and progressive usefulness to their "operative" or functional character – that is, when they are coupled with effective fortitude and action. Given this more pragmatic account of ideals, Kopelman's position can be charitably reinterpreted as arguing for the only "true" ideal that makes sense – the ideal that is achievable given the situation at hand. Read this way, Kopelman has done a great service to the use of the concept of "best interest."

Now, when we recognize that our ideals must come as practically conceived, we are confronted with the need to adjudicate many competing ideals – that wide array of issues and interests that the situation and those involved calls forth. Not only do children live with and because of others; those others are constrained, affected, influenced, and beholden to their communities, cultures, states, and so forth. To see this, it is helpful to analyze "interests" identifying several operative "types" of interests at play when making decisions for children.

An analysis of the everyday concept of "interest" shows that we use the term in at least four ways (from Dewey 1985 [1916], 132–133). First, we might use "interest" to apply to *that which we actively pursue* – "She is interested in soccer; she plays it every day, and watches it on TV often." Second, we say that someone has an "interest" in something when that *something affects his or her pursuits* – "He has an interest in the Iraq War because his daughter is in the Marine Corps." Third, we might apply the term "interest" to situations in which *our attitude is absorbed by our efforts or affections* – "He is clearly interested in the violin; when he plays, it is as if nothing matters to him." Fourth, we might also speak of something being "in one's interest." That is, apart from any individual's beliefs or practices, there may be a sense in which something matters to that individual's well-being that even she is unaware of or unconcerned with.

In the case of most adults (and many minors), we may rightly say that any of these four meanings of "interest" can apply. In particular, adults facing end-of-life decisions may have interests in the first sense – interests in religion, politics, economic or relational change or improvement – that are implicated in and by the decisions at hand. They may have interests in the second sense – interests in medical procedures suggested, costs of medical care – because they touch significantly on their lives. And they may own interests in the third sense – interests in music, art, craft, or scholarship – that which has been or will be lost or altered depending on the course of care. In the final sense of "being in one's interest," whatever this may be is left up to the adult herself to determine, as long as she has decisional capacity. The narrative emphasis throughout this book attempts to capture the importance of understanding and helping create a patient's life story specifically in light of how the first three senses of "interest" are best understood by and for the patient.

And yet infants, as already discussed, are at a stage in development – no matter their medical conditions – where we can be acceptably suspect about how these meanings of "interest" apply to them.[12] Quite simply, interests of the first and third sort do not apply to neonates, as long as we confine ourselves to speaking in terms of "having" or "owning" interest, and not in terms of "acquiring" or "developing" interests. That is, while many infants have the potential for interests of the first and third type, as neonates, those

---

[12] It is such conditions of the infant, and specifically severely impaired neonates, that is also the reason I do not take up consideration here of Ross's more teleological constraint for parental authority – promoting the "long-term autonomy" of the child.

interests are simply not yet actualized. And more narrowly, for some severely impaired neonates, the potential for interests of those sorts is not there either (this, admittedly, is a general claim that will apply unevenly at the level of the individual infant). This leaves us, primarily, with understanding neonatal interest as those of the second or fourth types – namely, interests as defined by those conditions, actions, or events that affect our own pursuits or some interests (we know not what) that apply beyond one's actions or intentions. "Interests" in these two senses are related, for while conditions and events often obtain beyond our efforts or without our approval, they apply to neonates insofar as the decisions made and the care provided are not *with* the neonate (only *about* her) and they directly affect the well-being of the child now and the future possibilities for the child later.

While this analysis of interests reduces to a fairly narrow set of meanings when looked at according to the current state of the infant's experience, analyzed in another way, the range of interests and what we might call "interest sources" in neonatal care is wide indeed. That is, when analyzed not according to conceptual meaning but in terms of the sources from which interests arise, the number of categories for consideration expands greatly. In fact, the breadth of interests (qualified by source) that are often brought to bear in decision making for newborns makes any type of pragmatic best-interest determination quite complex indeed. A breakdown of interest-source types is given on page 141.[13]

---

[13] Of course, interests can be analyzed many different ways. It may be helpful to compare other analytical taxonomies. For example, Christine Harrison, in a talk to the Florida Bioethics Network in October 2008, suggested the following:

Interests of children generally:

- stable family relationships
- early bonding
- freedom from pain and suffering
- keeping the future open

Interests of this child:

- specific fears
- sources of suffering
- future goals
- culture, religion, values of family

Possible interests *of* a newborn (i.e., what might be *of interest to* a newborn):

- Medical interests: treatment possibilities and prognosis (these would be determined by physicians, perhaps in conjunction with families)
- Pain/suffering interests: avoiding harm or indignity (these could be determined by almost anyone involved in the situation)
- Future-potential interests (of two types)
- What can be imagined for this child? (this question is captured by some combination of the others listed above and below when those interests are what Buchanan and Brock call "future-oriented" [1989, 247])
- What might this child want? (this question is a kind of epistemic issue – a guess at what the child would want if . . . ; we project and triangulate from our own experiences to fashion this, and frankly, it may be entirely nonsensical)

Possible interests *in* a newborn (i.e., who/what might be *interested in* a newborn):

- Communally imposed interests: cultural beliefs about the value of disabilities, concerns for dignity, respect, and so on
- Familial interests: affects on family, religious/cultural values of family, parental sensibilities
- State interests: protection of citizens from abuse or neglect

This list accounts for many (if not all) of the operative influencing interests, and even when in practice several of these interest sources are reducible to how they are manifested by parents and physicians (and even state social workers) at the bedside, it would be incorrect to say that we need only then consider the interests of the parents, the medical facts, and the delimitations of the state. Cultures and communities really do exist apart from how families incorporate those values, and pain and suffering occurs regardless of whether or not the state defines such pain and suffering as evidence of neglect or abuse. Buchanan and Brock are correct that what affects the child is singularly important to consider; Ross too is correct that the family is an intimate unit the interests of which should be addressed;

Diekema rightly captures the practical and emotional concerns for avoiding harm; and Kopelman recognizes the significance of aiming for a *practical telos* in decision making. Taken together, these accounts begin to develop a more robust, and I argue more accurate, picture of the child's interests – insofar as all of these become interests in and of the child.[14]

Of course, such a complex of interests is difficult to manage, and frankly some interests will only get lip service rather than deep consideration, and yet have we done a thorough ethical deliberation if any one of these interests has not been accounted for in some way? I would argue that we have not, and further, where possible, a story that can be told that satisfies all interests involved is better than one that cannot – the more inclusive the better. Thus, I recommend just that – that we attempt to develop storylines, narratives creatively determined that attempt to bring together all the interests at play, and not just defer to parents as the "rightful" decision makers, not only to the law as the limit on decision, nor restrictively to medicine as "objectively" and "dispassionately" correct.

The Role of Parenting in Decision-Making

To accomplish this, Western social convention favors making the parents primary authors, and yet this social convention is misleading. Parent do have a unique relationship with their children, a relationship of concern and obligation, of responsibility and intimacy that does not fall on any other persons or groups in our society. And yet this does not mean that parents are anointed with the sole power of authorship over their child's life – nor for that matter, is any other single entity or institution so authorized *a priori*. Instead, the relationship of parent to child does require that the story of the infant's care and the decision making that occurs should allow the parents, in particular, to confirm that their interests have been taken seriously.

---

[14] Of course, there are a great many more discussions of "interests" in medicine with emphases placed on such concepts as "community" (see Emanuel and Emanuel 1993) or familial relationship (not just parents) (see Nelson and Nelson 1995), among others.

In this way, any situation in which medical decisions about a severely impaired infant do not demonstrate the serious consideration of the interests of the parents is *prima facie* suspect. But, again, let us be clear about why would this be, and whether this is true of any other set of interests listed earlier.

It is not new to recount reasons why parents play a privileged role in the decisions made about their children. As Hilde and James Nelson point out, "Family members are stuck with each other" (1995, 101) and "Intimacy produces special responsibilities" (102). Alternately, using the three meanings of "interest" from before, there is no doubt that *parents in their roles as parents* are actively interested – that is, they are *parenting*; further, the decisions made for and about their children are of interest to the parent – they touch and affect the parents themselves; and finally, there can be the deep personal investment of a parent in a child – the effect of absorption into the role of parent to this child. The role of parent, more so than any other role, is readily situated to take on all three of these senses of 'interest' in relation to her child. Nothing in the radically empirical attitude – that is, in the careful consideration of the complexity of operative interests – adds to this fact, nor does it add to the consequent common acceptance that this intimate relationship between parents and children places parents in a position of authority and responsibility. At most, radical empiricism, with its emphasis on experience as it comes, strengthens the account of *prima facie* familial intimacy, since experience (as we have already noted) demonstrates that we are socially situated beings, and no social relationship is more significant to the infant than to her parents – at least not initially. In most (though certainly not all) cases, the story of being a parent does not end with the birth of a child, but only begins there. Thus, the story of parenthood is predicated on the existence and well being of progeny. No two stories, it would seem, are any more closely related than that of parent and child – with the effects of one potentially affecting the course of the other dramatically, and often (spousal relations can demonstrate a similar intimacy and significance, which is why the traditional presumption of "next of kin" decision making goes to the spouse first).

Of course, it is worth asking whether or not neonates (and severely impaired ones at that) are morally unique regarding these considerations. That is, in what ways, if any, do neonates differ from other children – toddlers, adolescents, disabled teens – in this "radically empirical" consideration of interests? Is it not also the case that parental interests have presumptive force for any child, or do other interests begin to gain weight and force in our considerations?

It is surely the case that for all minors, both the law and common morality already accept the presumption of parental authority. Ross clearly argues that the relationship of parents to children leads to a significant amount of moral authority – constrained, but operative. Diekema's own take on the harm principle, while setting forth the conditions under which the state has a right to intervene in decision making for children, has the purposeful effect of protecting the space in which parental authority should be allowed to hold sway. The examples can be multiplied with other accounts of the issues we have been discussing, but what is significant about the radically empirical account herein is not one of a new direction but of a required awareness and emphasis – namely, that parental authority in decision making, while rightly presumptive, is not exhaustive of a child's interests. Rather than addressing limits of authority or threshold conditions that must be met or avoided, the emphasis throughout this chapter is first on recognizing all the interests at play, and only then we can begin to address adequately the complexity of the situation.

However, what makes the neonatal period unique, and what severe impairment brings into stark relief, is that the decisions made are for beings whose development is so immature, so inexperienced, and potentially *always* will be, that the "interests" under consideration are never those expressed by the patient. The patient is of such an age and intellect that *her* personality is unformed, *her* interests are unavailable – that is, to repeat, her very *self* has yet to be determined. This places the entire moral burden for decision making elsewhere – on parents, on healthcare providers, even on the state to a degree. Again, our decisions are not with, but about, severely impaired neonates.

And those decisions require high degrees of speculation, while the physical impairments themselves disrupt our speculations. What kind of life will the child potentially lead? What level of impairment will the child be able to endure? How will she get along in the world if impairment is chronic? Unless we ourselves have experience with (or concerning) such impairments, our decisions typically begin from what we consider to be "normal" human development; we look to ourselves and others as the paradigms to be achieved in and through the development processes of the child. And yet her life may simply not "fit" into our conception of "normal." To compound the speculative frustrations, unlike for disabled adolescents, we have no life history of the neonate to draw upon for our decisions – no expression of desires, no patterned emotive responses, no conversation. Thus, I reiterate, we are left with a myriad conditions and interests that affect our decision making about this infant.

Will some interests rise above others? Certainly. In many (maybe even most) cases, parental interests will have a weighted precedence to them. In some cases, state interests may intervene. In others, medical facts will delimit the options; while in still others, cultural practices will influence the direction in which to go. In fact, if I can be so infuriating to those who have argued for their positions so carefully, it seems clear that each position has given us some insight to take away, while none has exhausted all possible reasonable approaches to neonatal care. Buchanan and Brock remind us that the being most significantly affected is the neonatal patient herself. Ross rightly emphasizes, among other things, the role of parental authority and familial interests. Diekema gives us a guiding principle for when state interests become determinatively significant. Kopelman keeps any "best interest" determination grounded practically to the conditions at hand. Radical empiricism, then, implies that the insights of each may be brought to bear, after recognizing, first, what interests are in fact at play.

Without any more of a guiding principle than, say, James's suggestion to "invent some manner" of satisfying all the relevant interests (James [1891], 623), this take on an approach to neonatal decision making will not satisfy some. And yet, I would argue, there is no stronger claim that can be made here that is neither question begging nor unduly restrictive to the complexities of experience. To capture these complexities and avoid both logical and practical pitfalls, what is required is a participatory process, one that seeks to include voices, puts interests and reasons into the fray, and works through them collaboratively – and all of this in light of the fact that the decisions about the neonate herself do not include her voice. Thus, while the interests come from many sources, the scope of reasonable options to be considered must recognize that it is the patient who cannot speak who is most significantly affected in the process.

Caring for Neonates at the End of Life

The infant patient, without a voice of her own, thus poses unique circumstances in which decision making must occur. While I have argued that there are good reasons to support parents as primary decision makers, I have also placed emphasis on the fact that a myriad other interest sources exists, and we ignore or minimize their significance, not only at our peril, but truly at the peril of the neonate. And yet, particularly when discussing infants born with severe impairments or at the limits of viability (to the extent that technology cannot support vitality), are there circumstances, conditions, decisions, or actions that act as either limiting factors or are beyond the pale of morality? That is, do some conditions and situations require particular actions, regardless of the wishes of particular parties in the fray?

For example, it has been argued that neonatologists should not attempt to resuscitate extremely premature infants (less than or equal to twenty-two weeks gestation – Nuffield 2006). Others have argued that anencephaly also merits no medical therapy for the purpose of sustaining the infant's life (cf. Baby K case). This list of comorbidities and conditions might be multiplied, but the point is that some believe that there are neonatal conditions that do not warrant medically aggressive care.

In fact, based on concerns raised by Montell and Lantos (2002; cf. Lantos 2001, ch. 10), John Paris (et al. 2006a, b) claims that under such extreme neonatal conditions, it is morally troubling to offer treatment options to parents as this places an undue decision-making burden on them. Drawing from literature (Dostoevsky, specifically),

Paris et al. argue that literature, much more compellingly than philosophy, demonstrates that in "live experience" we learn that

A parental decision to terminate treatment on a child is not the rational calculus of balancing burdens and benefits. . . . Such situations – overlaid with feelings of guilt, rage, and inadequacy – are not readily subjected to rational analysis. Nor are they perceived as an opportunity to exercise personal choice. They are, at best, an awful and unwelcome burden. (2006a, 390; cf. 2006b 149)

At first glance, such a suggestion runs directly counter to the thirty-year tradition of requiring physicians to gain *informed* consent from patients/parents. Presumably, this is done in light of the "unwelcome burden" of decision making, relieving parents of having to "sign a death warrant for their child" (Paris et al. 2006a 390). The compelling aspects of this position must not be overlooked. First, it would seem that there are severe neonatal conditions that truly do not warrant anything other than comfort/palliative care. Second, it is certainly the case that some parents (maybe even most, for all we know) are *unduly* overwhelmed with information, options, and consequent choices. Third, if we can identify particular parental decision makers who would be burdened by being given quite vacuous options, we would be morally remiss in putting them in a position to have to choose when no "real" choice exists.

However, it is clear that two characteristics of a given situation must obtain for us to be confident in our moral footing: (1) We must be confident in our prognosis, and (2) we must know something about the parents with whom we are working. If our evidence is sufficiently strong (and it is important to note that little consensus has been gained concerning what constitutes sufficiently strong evidence), then the primary ingredient for Paris's argument exists. However, the question of "authorship" still remains – namely, what role should parents play in the authorship of their infant's life and death? What constitutes morally acceptable interactions with parents in order to make them participants, not afterthoughts, in their child's care? The only acceptable answer, given the arguments throughout this book, is open communication – early (perhaps even before some medical facts are known) and often (providing flexibility for decision-making under changing conditions) – about what the goals of care for the child are – what the parents desire *and why they desire it*, along with what physicians propose *and why they propose it*. Starting with conversations about the parents' interests allows physicians to consider their proposals in light of those values, not just the physical/medical conditions of the infant. Such consideration *may* then eventuate in the kind of discussion and decision limiting that Paris et al. suggest but that may not always occur.[15] And none of this requires, *a priori*, that the physicians do whatever the parents desire (see Chapter 5 on the discussion of goals of care), but it does require that conversations intended to open a participatory space for parents be initiated.

And yet even if the arguments that some have put forth concerning what physicians should *not* be required to do (under particular conditions) win the day, we are left to determine what then might be an appropriate response to caring for severely impaired infants so long as they are alive. That is, even if we all agree that certain conditions warrant a non-aggressive approach to treatment, such that we will aim instead at providing a good death for these children, what constitutes appropriate medical care for these dying patients?

---

[15] It is worth noting, but will not be discussed here, that there are some severe maladies of infants that have engendered the opposite response for some physicians. For example, hypoplastic left heart syndrome (HLHS) is a fatal condition if left untreated, and is associated with many co-morbidities even when treated. In fact, the "treatment" for HLHS is a series of three surgical procedures, the first of which (the Norwood procedure) must be performed within days of birth (the other two occurring over a period of many months thereafter). The Norwood procedure has been in existence for about twenty-five years, and adjustments to the surgical and post-surgical practices have been made such that pediatric cardiac centers report anywhere from 50–90 percent success (that is, 10–50 percent mortality) for HLHS patients. In light of these statistics (and especially at centers with the highest success rates), some physicians have argued that the option for allowing parents to choose "comfort care" for these children upon birth is unacceptable, and should not be offered (cf. Kon, Ackerson, & Lo 2004). Others believe that given both the mortality rates and the co-morbid factors associated with HLHS, "comfort care" remains a morally acceptable option and as such must be offered to all parents as a matter of satisfying ethically acceptable informed consent and shared decision making (cf. Kon 2005; Byrne & Murphy 2005). Parents themselves are divided, with more and more opting for surgical intervention, but still a critical number choosing comfort care (cf. Ross and Frader 2009).

Specifically, is such a practice as euthanasia[16] acceptable, even morally required, in some cases?

Revisiting Palliation and Goals of Care

On the specific question of euthanizing newborns, current controversy has been stirred by the so-called Groningen protocol (Verhagen and Sauer 2005a, b) from The Netherlands.[17] The Groningen protocol suggests that euthanizing infants who have a "hopeless prognosis [and] experience what parents and medical experts deem to be unbearable suffering" is morally acceptable when "parents and physicians are convinced that . . . death would be more humane than continued life" (2005a, 959–60). It should not be surprising that such a suggestion proved controversial. Aside from the general moral stance that "the direct taking of human life crosses a major boundary line" (Jotkowitz and Glick 2006, 157) – a concern that I have already argued is not necessarily true *a priori* – there remains the concern that euthanizing practices of newborns occur not because they are good medical practice but because "[a]ccess to pediatric palliation is poor, even in countries with first-class medical systems" (Murphy and Pritchard 2005, 2354). This observation is not new, and though lack of palliative care services still persists in adult end-of-life care facilities, it is the case that palliative care for children is running years behind its adult counterpart.

It is in this context of arguments for euthanasia of newborns and a call for better pediatric palliative care that we must remember that the decisions we are making for severely impaired newborns are vital – literally life and death. Previously, under analogous vital conditions, I argued that while the life stories of some adults may call forth (upon investigation and reflection) moral obligations to

---

[16] It is worth remembering that "euthanasia" here does not encompass acts of withholding or withdrawing life-sustaining measures, but only so-called "active" measured of hastening death (medication overload, and so on). Though withholding and withdrawing have not been included in the definition of "euthanasia" throughout the book, some other texts conflate these issues.

[17] This was followed in November 2006 by a request from Britain's Royal College of Obstetrics and Gynecology for a parliamentary debate in support of the practice of euthanizing the "sickest newborns."

aid their dying processes (possibly through assisted suicide or even euthanasia), can the same be said for neonates whose life stories are only now beginning to be written and who have no authorship abilities of their own? In fact, I would argue, unlike in the case of adults – even incapacitated adults – aid in the dying processes of children should be focused on palliative practices. The primary reason for this position arises from what it is that makes neonates unique – the fact that decision making is always about, and not with, them. As Alex Kon (2007) has argued, the problem is that so many of our determinations as to whether or not to euthanize a newborn are based solely on "subjective" considerations of an infant's "suffering." As Kon puts it, "In contrast to adults, infants are unable to communicate their personal experience of suffering. Because we cannot know the infant's subjective experience, and therefore can accurately judge neither the amount of her suffering nor the balance of the benefits and burdens of her life, we can never be certain that an individual act of hastening the death of a neonate is truly an act of euthanasia" (458). Kon concludes, "Further research in Pediatric Palliative Medicine will assist physicians and parents in caring for such infants, and hopefully will alleviate the suffering of most, if not all, children with chronic illnesses" (460).

Additionally, palliative care is compatible not only with decisions to forego life-sustaining measures as well as orders not to resuscitate, but also with many types of continued curative/aggressive measures. That is, palliative care allows for flexibility in decision making, and that flexibility is required given that the interests we are attempting to fulfill are, as has already been discussed, not of the child's own making/choosing/developing. So, again, the moral case for championing palliative care for neonatal end of life comes from the reality that neonates are not participants, in the usual sense, in their own care.

As a historical fact, palliative care for children is still fairly new, running even behind adult palliative care, which is itself relatively new to medicine. This is in part the case because there was a long medical prejudice that very young children do not experience pain to the same degree as more developed persons. Some even believed that late-term fetuses and newborns did not feel any pain. This belief has been undermined by a good deal of evidence and research (Puchalski and Hummel 2002; Grunau 2002; Lee SJ et al. 2005). Now, promoting palliative care for children is getting a significant push (cf. Himelstein et al. 2004; IOM 2002).

While best left to more comprehensive texts to discuss (cf. Carter & Levetown 2004), palliative care can be briefly described as a comprehensive approach to pain and suffering – medical, emotional, even spiritual. No longer confined strictly to end-of life considerations, palliative care runs throughout good medical practices. No doubt, however, palliative care services, hospice, and other practices do have a significant role in end-of life care. As Joe Fins has argued, good palliative practices must focus on the goals of care. This reminds us of the recurring theme from previous chapters that the radically empirical attitude moves us to focus on the complexity of interests at play in any given situation, attempting to bring these complexities into focus and under control through fostering "a mutual understanding about disease trajectory and what goals of care might be appropriate given the changing medical facts and . . . family preferences" (Fins 2006, 86; cf. Kopleman AE 2006).

In previous chapters, the argument for a deep narrative understanding of the trajectory of life-stories was the support from which decisions arose to forego life-sustaining treatments, even to engage in physician assisted death. Thus, when adults can participate in the authorship of their final chapters, they should be encouraged to do so – that is, they should be made participants in their care. When adults cannot participate because they lack decisional capacity, it might still be possible to project end-of-life decisions that are consistent with the experiences, values, and interests of these dying adult through careful consideration of their life stories to-date. However, at no time has it been argued that end-of-life care should include euthanizing measures that cannot be reasonably projected from an adult patient's life story. In fact, under conditions in which a patient's interests are significantly unknown, caution and reticence about such actions are warranted, though palliation and ceasing life-sustaining measures may be appropriate given the medical conditions.

By analogy, neonates are beings with no significant life-story of their own to draw upon.[18] As has been said, the interests at play are not ones neonates "own" themselves, but are ones projected on them from others. Thus it follows that caution and reticence in euthanizing practices is warranted. In other words, while palliation and hospice may be noted as options for care with dying adults, such measures for dying children, as already mentioned, are not simply one option among several. Palliative care at the end of life is always appropriate for newborns when the decision to cease aggressive treatment has been made.

What this requires, however, is much better medical understanding of how to relieve the pain and suffering of children, stronger support systems within hospitals for caregivers and families, a greater acceptance by physicians to trigger these services early enough to make a positive difference in the dying process, and smoother social and economic processes and considerations (i.e., state laws or insurance coverage) (cf. Himelstein, et al. 2004, 1757–60; IOM 2002). All three of these areas are still lacking in many facilities. As mentioned, "[a]ccess to pediatric palliation is poor, even in countries with first-class medical systems" (Murphy and Pritchard 2005, 2354), and as noted in Chapter 3, until the institutional, environmental, and practical conditions that are necessary to provide good palliative care unto death are established, it is difficult to deny that physician-assisted dying for (most likely) a small number of infants may be preferable as a means of providing a good death. This realization should supply the necessary motivation for those who are aghast at such a possibility to get to work on closing the gap in providing good palliative care.

At bottom, however, palliative care, as Chris Feudtner (2007) has nicely argued, should be a process of collaborative communication among caregivers (parental, medical, and otherwise). Whatever decisions are to be made, or problems to be solved, they must be done

---

[18] There are some important nuances here to consider: Since we are not insular beings, but constitutively social, every newborn is already born into the ongoing stories of the communities that care and embrace her. The point, however, is that the individuality of any particular newborn does not initially arise internally from out of the newborn, but is imposed externally from those story sources of family, community, culture, and so on.

collaboratively – or, in my terminology, in partnership. Given that the story of a patient's living and dying is not hers alone, authorship is at best a shared enterprise. The goals of care are shaped by parental hopes and medical abilities, all this in light of the given conditions of the child – this three-way complex occurs within social-cultural structures and norms. Thus, not only the particulars of our radical "interest-source" taxonomy but general operations of radical empiricism push us not simply to hear from others but to work with them to fashion the best outcomes for the child. If I read Feudtner correctly, then, radical empiricism becomes manifest as collaborative communication in and through palliative care, making palliative care a constitutive aspect of end-of-life care for all neonates (and, frankly, all persons).

A Word about Non-infant Minors and End-of-Life Decision Making

While this chapter has focused exclusively on neonates (and even more pointedly on severely impaired newborns), there is of course much more to the story of end-of-life care with children. Pre-teens and adolescents die too, and their care at the end of life has moral significance as well.

It is probably not necessary to discuss all possible developmental issues with children given the arguments throughout this book – the reader, I suspect, can extrapolate the arguments given thus far. Briefly, the radically empirical position requires us not to devalue children's participation in their care too hastily. Certainly, as children grow and gain experiences, they become more significant authors of their own stories. Recent evidence continues to support the idea that children who have experience with healthcare issues can, even at young ages, demonstrate reasonable decision making about their care (cf. Alderson et al. 2006). As a mater of suggested policy, which has now been enacted in a great number of institutions, the American Association of Pediatrics (AAP) has tried to capture the significance of childhood development to decision making by proposing that for very young children (say, younger than the age of seven), assent from them in medical (and research) decision making is not necessary. For pre-adolescent children (between seven and fourteen, or so), assent of some kind is appropriate, and with adolescents (approximately older than fourteen), dissent should be honored (AAP 1995). This developmental insight is not new, and the implications for care of older children are obvious – namely, to the extent possible, children should participate in their care and in care decisions. Life is a continuum of growth, learning, and development, and as far as possible, we should each be allowed to make of our worlds what we want.

There are moral, social, psychological, and other practical restrictions, of course. Lainie Ross argues that the AAP went too far in supporting adolescent dissent, bothered specifically by the unwarranted conflation of decision-making capacity (she says "competence") with "health care decisionmaking autonomy" (Ross 1997, 42; cf. Ross 2008). And yet, as she also goes to great lengths to point out, "If there are cases in which the denial of a competent [sic.] child's dissent does not respect the child's developing and partially actualized personhood, then the competent [sic.] child's consent is necessary and his dissent must be binding" (1998, 67). Arising from Ross's positive constraint on parental authority, her argument is that parents are obligated to promote the long-term autonomy of their children, and as such, "parents [and others] do themselves and their children a big disservice if they fail to include their children in the decision-making process" (67). Ross suggests that including the child (at the very least) "serves both instrumental and intrinsic purposes" (67).

Ross's concern for including children can be put in the radically empirical language of this book (though, admittedly, she might not wish to go as far as I) – to take experience (*all* experience) seriously is to include, not exclude, the experience of children. Inclusion, however, is not agreement or acceptance; it is the taking seriously of the consequences of either following or ignoring the interests of children, and accounting for how they were considered in light of the decisions made. As children grow and their experiences mature, the importance of their concerns (now, more carefully considered) grows as well.

Along these lines, it would seem reasonable to provide better advance planning *with*, not just *for*, children, particularly those with early-onset chronic diseases. However, no state accepts as legally binding an advance directive for a minor, and much of the limited research about such planning has focused on parental attitudes, and not on the concerns of children themselves (cf. Hammes et al. 2005; Wharton et al. 1996). One study, though, has shown that adolescents can demonstrate the necessary decisional capacity and sufficient understanding of the complex issues in end-of-life planning (McAliley et al. 2000). As mentioned, the AAP has for more than a decade advocated a developmental approach to the inclusion of children in decision making (AAP 1995).

In sum, my stance is this: Inclusion of developing children's interests makes them participants in care that is about and for *them*. Exclusion sets aside their experiences, treating them as invaluable to the process of decision-making (cf. Blustein 2009; Clayton 2009, among many others). It is, after all, their life stories that are most centrally affected, and while those stories are significantly intertwined with the stories of their family members, communities, and even medicine itself, children have a unique stake in their own care, and they are best served whenever we demonstrate that we recognize that fact by helping them to participate in their own care and the path their lives will take.

7

Caring for Patients

Cure, Palliation, Comfort, and Aid in the Process of Dying

> Language is made up of physical existences; sound, or marks on paper. . . . But these do not *operate* or function as mere physical things when they are media of communication. They operate in virtue of the *representative* capacity or *meaning*. . . . The convention or common consent which sets [language] apart as a means of recording and communicating meaning is that of agreement in action; of shared modes of responsive behavior and participation in their consequences.
>
> *John Dewey*

With each succeeding chapter, I have added one tool or insight after another. In Chapter 2, we developed an understanding of the radically empirical attitude that takes all and only experience seriously. This led to an understanding that selves are social products best understood, not as isolated beings, but in light of their rich, ongoing life stories. In Chapter 3, we took these insights and moved to a pragmatic understanding of obligations that arise from taking all interests seriously, eventuating in the urging to "invent some manner of satisfying" as many demands as possible. The result of such intelligent invention (or inquiry) is what we called a moral obligation. Chapter 4 focused on patients with decisional capacity at the end of life, and placed an emphasis on making decisions that help the patient author her life story while she is dying, recognizing that for some few individuals this might mean that others are morally obligated to help them die. Chapter 5 turned to those who were permanently or significantly decisionally incapacitated, and argued that advance directives should be taken as attempts to extend the patient's authorship of her own story, and where absent surrogates should attempt to sensitively craft the patient's narrative in the context of the patient's values, and not in isolation but through collaboration. Because of the severity and complexity of the conditions of PVS and MCS, in particular, conflict among invested parties (surrogates with each other or surrogates with healthcare professionals) can occur, and it was suggested that physicians should not speculate but take a direct and careful focus on goals of care from the perspective of the surrogate in light of the patient and the medical considerations necessary. In Chapter 6, we looked at the significant moral differences between adults and infants, and elucidated the importance of identifying operative interests.

Throughout this book I have argued that dying is a process within lived experience. Individuals themselves are socially situated beings whose interests arise as part of a history and culture and feedback into the communities of which they are a part. Physicians and other healthcare professionals encounter dying patients during these processes, and I have argued they should work to make their patients participants in their own care. While "participation" looks very different for each patient, and even seems paradoxical for some, the narrative of lived experience, of families and communities, helps ground various modes of participation.

Caring for dying patients is no easy task, and the arguments, while developed to help in everyday circumstances, may in fact help more on the margins of practice. Everyday clinical practice is, first and foremost, focused on caring for the patient, and as a default, this typically results in aggressive, curative measures – treatments designed to fight or stave off illness, mend injury, and avoid death. We have noted that not all patients want or need this kind of medical attention, and of course this is not a new insight. Healthcare professionals have known this for generations, and yet their training and habits lead them to what we might call "curative care" almost instinctively.

In fact, arguments are then made as to why such aggressive measures are necessary, even over the objections of a patient who does not desire them. The arguments are often morally charged, and this book has tried to demonstrate that these arguments do not always hold the ethical water they claim, and in fact other acts of caring – through aid in dying – can be morally appropriate for some patients.

For many who resist this latter move but also resist the former, palliative care has been put forth as the morally appropriate alternative. I argued in Chapter 4 that while this can be a useful alternative for some dying adult patients, not all patient situations will be morally fulfilled by this alternative. In Chapter 6, I went further in support of palliative care as a strong moral approach to dying children. It was in that discussion that I tried to define palliative care, and did so in a way that made palliative care an option not wholly isolatable from some curative care practices.

In this final chapter, I will make a case for clarifying some terms and concepts often used in the care of dying patients. What frequently occurs at the end of life in hospitals is confusion among staff and in communication with patients/families about what our terms and practices mean. In particular, medical professionals have embraced the phrase "comfort care" to denote something concerning end-of-life care with some patients. However, asking five healthcare professionals what "comfort care" entails will most likely produce five different answers. What I want to argue is that "comfort care" is best viewed as an approach to the care of dying patients, an approach that marks a shift away from curative care. As such, I think it a mistake to describe "comfort care" as an "order" or as equivalent to DNR or withdrawal of life-sustaining measures. Instead, "comfort care" indicates that the broad goals of care are decidedly focused on the best possible dying processes, making decisions that use medicine and its technologies to ease patients at the ends of their lives.

By both tradition and necessity, medical personnel approach new-patient care with the attitude that they should attempt to cure the patient's illness or injury. This makes perfect sense, of course. Medicine is a problem-solving activity, and solutions typically mean eradication of ailments. That is often why patients come to see healthcare professionals, and as a consequence why technology, research, and medication are developed.

However, I have mentioned earlier, and argued elsewhere (Hester 2001), that the goal of medical encounters should be healthy living, even (perhaps "especially") for those in the process of dying. Thus, while the default approach to patient care is curative ("aggressive") care, such an approach does not exhaust medical responsibilities. Not all patients can be cured, and yet many who cannot be cured can still have healthy dying processes. In my view, medicine is required to apply its tools, skills, and knowledge in ways that help even those patients for whom a cure is not possible and the dying process has begun.

Caring for these dying patients takes more than knowledge and skills, however; it necessarily takes a shift in our approach to care that moves away from a focus on the goal of cure to what, as I have said earlier, many call "comfort care." Comfort care marks a change in attitude, a shift in focus – new goals and opportunities. Of course, we could give this shift in focus any number of names, but I believe "comfort care" can do the work, and has not yet gathered enough other baggage to anchor it to other possible meanings.

"Comfort care," as I argue, can be seen, not in contrast to, but standing alongside, curative care as a way of arranging our decisions concerning medical care planning for patients. The discussions we have and the orders to be given, then, are done specifically with the idea that they feed into the goal of comfort in dying, and not cure or prolongation. So, just as we would discuss and possibly chose aggressive chemotherapy for a patient who wants to try to rid herself of cancer, we would talk about and possibly stop the use of, say, a Bi-pap mask for someone who finds it uncomfortable and is no longer trying to stave off death. That is, *each option we provide and each choice made is made with the goal of comfort, not cure.*

What this also entails, then, is that no single order denotes a move to comfort care. That puts the cart before the horse. Neither cessation of invasive ventilation nor the writing of DNR orders is in itself comfort care. Instead, such decisions should be made in light of the kind of care (that is, the goals of care) to be pursued. Of course, considerations of DNR orders probably trigger a shift (even if not wholly considered) in the direction of care, but the purpose of such a trigger should be to answer the question: What are the goals of care, and if DNR is a consideration, should we then be thinking of a complete shift of attitude toward "comfort"?

Note here that "comfort" is also not equivalent to "palliative." As I have said, palliative care can conjoin with curative care, and would also be appropriate (perhaps even necessary) in comfort care.

I present a modified Venn diagram here to illustrate what I'm proposing:

SPHERES OF CARE

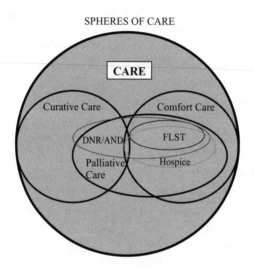

DEFINITIONS

Curative Care:	primary focus on providing treatments intended to eradicate or diminish the effects of disease, injury, or illness
Comfort Care:	primary focus on providing treatments and support that provide comfort during the dying process.
Palliative Care:	specific focus on caring for the pain and suffering (physical and emotional) of patients and their support systems
DNR/AND:	Do Not Resuscitate/Allow Natural Death
FLST:	Forego Life-sustaining Treatments

POINTS OF INTEREST
- Palliative Care is broader than Comfort Care
- DNR orders may exist even when other curative measures continue
- FLST entails Comfort Care and DNR orders
- Though atypical, hospice does not always require FLST
- Comfort Care allows a limited use of curative measures for the purpose of palliation

The diagram emphasizes that what medicine is enjoined to provide first and foremost is *care*. Whether focused primarily on cure, palliation, or comfort, care is the bedrock of medical practice. At the same time, physicians want flexibility in developing care plans. Even more importantly, the individuality of patients requires flexibility. This view of cure, comfort, and palliation is developed precisely with that flexibility in mind. Individual orders should match the individual goals of specific patients and their dying processes.

What I did not add, even though my arguments throughout merit it, is a space in the diagram for active aid in dying – from PAS to morally legitimate euthanasia. Even good moral argument (if that is what I have provided) does not wipe away the controversy so easily, and thus I leave the diagram flexible enough to be able to add it as moral arguments begin to prevail in the public ethos.

The points made here are made specifically to help clarify our use of terminology that so far has little settled usage. Clarification matters, since only then can good communication follow. Communication among team members, and especially with patients and families, is central to making everyone participants in the patient's care.

As patients move through the dying process, our care for and about them must keep them in mind – not cookie-cutter care, but sensitive to their life stories and to those of their families and the communities of which they are a part. Taking seriously a radically empirical approach to patient care that encompasses patient experiences as integral to medical decision making, and helping to provide the space and tools for development of the final chapters in the lives of dying patients, is a morally significant act that we must continually take seriously, vigilant in our attempts to create some manner in which a peaceful death can prevail.

Works Cited

Alderson P, Sutcliffe K, and **Curtis K**. 2006. Children's Competence to Consent to Medical Treatment. *Hastings Center Report*, **36**(6):25–34.

American Academy of Pediatrics (AAP): Committee on Bioethics. 1995. Informed Consent, Parental Permission, and Assent in Pediatric Practice." *Pediatrics*, **95**:314–7.

Andrews K et al. 1996. Misdiagnosis of the Vegetative State: Retrospective Study in a Rehabilitation Unit. *British Medical Journal*, **313**:13–6.

Arras JD. 1984. Towards an Ethic of Ambiguity. *Hastings Center Report*, **14**(2):25–33.

—— 1997. Physician-Assisted Suicide: A Tragic View. *Journal of Contemporary Health Law and Policy*, **13**:361–89, and in **Battin, Rhodes**, and **Silvers** 1998, 279–300.

Asch A. 2005. Recognizing Death while Affirming Life: Can End-of-Life Reform Uphold a Disabled Person's Interest in Continued Life? In *Improving End of Life Care: A Hastings Center Special Report*. **Jennings B**, **Kaebnick GE**, and **Murray TH** (eds.), S31–36.

Avesani R, Gambini MG, and **Albertini G**. 2006. The Vegetative State: A Report of Two Cases with a Long-Term Follow-Up. *Brain Injury*, **20**(3): 333–8.

Baird R and **Rosenbaum S** (eds.). 1989. *Euthanasia: The Moral Issues*. Prometheus Books.

Battin MP. 1994. *The Least Worst Death: Essays in Bioethics on the End of Life*. Oxford University Press.

—— 2005. *Ending Life: Ethics and the Way We Die*. Oxford University Press.

—— **Rhodes R** and **Silvers A**. 1998. *Physician-Assisted Suicide*. Routledge.

Baumrin B. 1998. Physician, Stay Thy Hand! In **Battin, Rhodes**, and **Silvers** 1998, 177–81.

Beauchamp T (ed.). 1996. *Intending Death*. Prentice Hall.

Beauchamp T and **Childress J**. 1996. *The Principles of Biomedical Ethics*, 4th edition, Oxford University Press. Also see 5th edition, 2001, and 6th edition, 2009.

Bellantoni L. 2003. What Good is a Pragmatic Bioethic? *Journal of Medicine and Philosophy*, **28**(5–6):615–34.

Benjamin M. 2003. Pragmatism and the Determination of Death. In **McGee** 2003, 193–206.

——— 2003. *Philosophy and This Actual World*. Rowman & Littlefield.

Berlin I. 1969. *Four Essays on Liberty*. Oxford University Press.

Berger JT et al. 2008. Surrogate Decision Making: Reconciling Ethical Theory and Clinical Practice, *Annals of Internal Medicine*, **149**(1):48–53.

Bernat JL. 2004. On Irreversibility as a Prerequisite for Brain Death Determination. In **Machado** and **Shewmon** 2004, 161–8.

Bernstein, JM. 1990. Self-Knowledge as Praxis: Narrative and Narration in Psychoanalysis. In *Narrative in Culture*. **Nash C** (ed.). Routledge.

Bliton M and **Finder S**. 2002. Traversing Boundaries: Clinical Ethics, Moral Experience, and Withdrawal of Life Supports." *Theoretical Medicine and Bioethics*, **23**:233–258.

Blustein J. 1999. Choosing for Others as Continuing a Life Story: The Problem of Personal Identity Revisited. *Journal of Law, Medicine & Ethics*, **27**: 20–31.

Blustein J. 2009. Response (to Ross 2009). *Cambridge Quarterly of Healthcare Ethics*, **18**(3):315–20.

Brody BA. 1999. How Much of the Brain Must Be Dead? In **Younger** 1999, 71–82.

Brody H. 1987/2003. *Stories of Sickness*, 1st/2nd edition. Oxford University Press.

Brown H. 2000. *William James on Radical Empiricism and Religion*. University of Toronto Press.

Buchanan A. 1989. The Treatment of Incompetents. In *Health Care Ethics: An Introduction*. **Reagan T** (ed.). Temple University Press, 215–38.

——— and **Brock D**. 1989. *Deciding for Others: The Ethics of Surrogate Decision Making*. Oxford University Press.

Buchanan JH. 1989. *Patient Encounters*. Henry Holt.

Burrell D and **Hauerwas S**. 1979. From System to Story: An Alternative Pattern for Rationality in Ethics. In *Why Narrative? Readings in Narrative Theology*. **Hauerwas S** and **Jones LG** (eds.). W.B. Eerdmans, 158–190.

Burt RA. 2005. The End of Autonomy. In *Improving End of Life Care: A Hastings Center Special Report*. **Jennings B, Kaebnick GE**, and **Murray TH** (eds.), S9–13.

Byock I. 1997. Physician-Assisted Suicide is *Not* an Acceptable Practice for Physicians. In **Weir** 1997, 107–35.

——— 2003. Rediscovering Community at the Core of the Human Condition and Social Covenant. *Access to Hospice Care: Expanding Boundaries, Overcoming Barriers: Hastings Center Supplement*. **Jennings B** et al. (eds.), S40–4.

Byrne PA and **Weaver WF**. 2004. "Brain Death" Is Not Death. In **Machado** and **Shewmon** 2004, 43–50.

Byrne PJ and **Murphy A**. 2005. Informed Consent and Hypoplastic Left Heart Syndrome. *Acta Paediatrica,* **94**(9):1171–5.

Callahan D. 1992. Self-Determination Run Amok. *Hastings Center Report* **22**:52–55.

—— 1994. Ad Hominem Run Amok: A Response to John Lachs. *Journal of Clinical Ethics.* **5**(1):13–5.

—— 1995. Terminating Life-Sustaining Treatment of the Demented. *Hastings Center Report,* **25**(6):25–31.

—— 2000. A Burden upon Others: A Response to John Hardwig. In **Hardwig** 2000, 139–45.

—— 2002. Reason, Self-Determination, and Physician-Assisted Suicide. In **Foley** and **Hendin** 2002, 52–68.

Capron AM. 1999. The Bifurcated Legal Standard for Determining Death: Does It Work? In **Younger** 1999, 117–136.

—— 2001. Brain Death – Well Settled yet Still Unresolved. *New England Journal of Medicine,* **344**(16), 1244–6.

Carter BS and **Leuthner SR**. 2002. Decision Making in the NICU – Strategies, Statistics, and "Satisficing." *Bioethics Forum,* **18**(3/4):7–15.

Carter BS and **Levetown M**, eds. 2004. *Palliative Care for Infants, Children, and Adolescents: A Practical Handbook.* Johns Hopkins University Press.

Centers for Disease Control (CDC). 2004. Deaths From 39 Selected Causes by Place of Death. http://www.cdc.gov/nchs/datawh/statab/unpubd/mortabs/gmwk307.htm.

Chambers T. 1999. *The Fiction of Bioethics: Cases as Literary Texts.* Routledge.

Charon R. 2006. *Narrative Medicine: Honoring the Stories of Illness.* Oxford University Press.

Childs NL and **Mercer WN**. 1996. Late Improvement of Consciousness after Post-Traumatic Vegetative State. *New England Journal of Medicine,* **334**:11, 24–5.

Churchill J. 1989 Advance Directives: Beyond Respect for Freedom. In **Hackler, Moseley**, and **Vawter** 1989, 171–9.

Churchill LR. 1979. Interpretations of Dying: Ethical Implications for Patient Care. *Ethics, Science, and Medicine,* **6**(4):211–22.

Clauss RP and **Nel WH**. 2006. Drug Induced Arousal from the Permanent Vegetative State. *NeuroRehabilitation,* **21**:23–8.

Clauss RP, Guldenpfennig WM, Nel HW, et al. 2000. Extraordinary Arousal from Semi-Comatose State on Zolpidem: A Case Study. South African Medical Journal, **90**:68–72.

Clayton EW. 2009. Response (to Ross 2009). *Cambridge Quarterly of Healthcare Ethics,* **18**(3):320–22.

Cohn F and **Lynn J**. A Duty to Care. In Hardwig 2000, 145–54.

—— 2002. Vulnerable People: Practical Rejoinders to Claims in Favor of Assisted Suicide. In **Foley** and **Hendin** 2002, 238–60.

Coleman D. 2002. *Not Dead Yet*. In **Foley** and **Hendin** 2002, 213–37.

Coleman GD. 1987. Assisted Suicide: An Ethical Perspective. *In Baird and Rosembaum*, 1989.

Coles Robert. 1989. *The Call of Stories: Teaching and the Moral Imagination*. Houghton Mifflin.

Cooper W. 2002. *The Unity of William James's Thought*. Vanderbilt University Press.

Cranford RE. 1988. The Persistent Vegetative State: The Medical Reality (Getting the Facts Straight). *Hastings Center Report*, **18**(1):27–32.

—— 1991. Helga Wanglie's Ventilator. *Hastings Center Report*, **21**(4):23–4.

—— 2002. What is the Minimally Conscious State? *Western Journal of Medicine*, **176**:129–30.

Dagi TF and **Kaufman R**. 2001. Clarifying the Discussion on Brain Death. *Journal of Medicine and Philosophy*, **26**(5):503–25.

Davidoff F. 2002. Lessons from the Dying. In **Snyder** and **Caplan** 2002, 98–105.

Dewey J. 1985 [1916]. *Democracy and Education*. Middle Works of John Dewey, 1899–1924, vol. 9. **Boydston J** (ed.). Southern Illinois University Press.

—— 1988 [1920]. *Reconstruction in Philosophy*. Middle Works of John Dewey, 1899–1924, vol. 12. **Boydston J** (ed.). Southern Illinois University Press, 77–201.

—— 1988 [1922]. *Human Nature and Conduct*. Middle Works of John Dewey, 1899–1924, vol. 14. **Boydston J** (ed.). Southern Illinois University Press.

Dewey, John and **Tufts, James**. 1989 [1932]. *Ethics*. Later Works of John Dewey, 1925–1953, vol. 7. **Boydston J** (ed.). Southern Illinois University Press.

—— 1991 [1939a]. *Theory of Valuation*. Later Works of John Dewey, 1925–1953. **Boydston J** (ed.). Southern Illinois University Press, 189–251.

—— 1991 [1939b]. *The Unity of the Human Being*. Later Works of John Dewey, 1925–1953. **Boydston J** (ed.). Southern Illinois University Press, 323–37.

Diekema DS. 2004. Parental Refusals of Medical Treatments: The Harm Principle as Threshold for State Intervention. *Theoretical Medicine and Bioethics*. **24**:243–64.

Dorland, WAN. 1994. *Dorland's Illustrated Medical Dictionary*, 28th edition, W.B. Saunders.

Dresser R. 1989. Advance Directives, Self-Determination, and Personal Identity. In **Hackler** et al. 1989, 155–70.

—— 1995. Dworkin on Dementia: Elegant Theory, Questionable Policy. *Hastings Center Report*, **25**(6):32–8.

Dubler NN. 2005. Conflict and Consensus at the End of Life. In *Improving End of Life Care: A Hastings Center Special Report*. **Jennings B**, **Kaebnick GE**, and **Murray TH** (eds.), S19–25.

—— and **Nimmons D**. 1992. *Ethics on Call*. Harmony Books.

Dworkin R. 1993. *Life's Dominion: An Argument about Abortion, Euthanasia, and Individual Freedom*. Alfred A. Knopf.

Emanuel EJ, Fairclough DL, and **Emanuel LL**. 2000. Attitudes and Desires Related to Euthanasia and Physician-Assisted Suicide among Terminally Ill Patients and Their Caregivers. *Journal of the American Medical Association,* **284**(19):2460–8.

Emanuel EJ, Fairclough DL, Daniels ER, and **Clarridge BR**. 1996. Euthanasia and Physician-Assisted Suicide: Attitudes and Experiences of Oncology Patients, Oncologists, and the Public. *Lancet,* **347**(9018):1805–10.

Emanuel LL and **Emanuel EJ**. 1993. Decisions at the End of Life: Guided by Communities of Patients. *Hastings Center Report,* 23(5):6–14.

Engelhardt HT. 1975. Ethical Issues in Aiding the Death of Young Children. In *Beneficent Euthanasia.* **Kohl M** (ed.). Prometheus Books.

—— 1986. *The Foundations of Bioethics.* Oxford University Press.

—— 1987. *Introduction.* In *Euthanasia and the Newborn.* **McMillan RC, Engelhardt TS**, and **Spicker SF** (eds.). Reidel.

Faber-Langendoen K and **Karlawish JHT**. 2002. Ought Physician-Assisted Suicide Be Only *Physician* Assisted? In **Snyder** and **Caplan** 2002, 44–54.

Facco E and **Machado C**. 2004. Evoked Potentials in Diagnosis of Brain Death. In **Machado** and **Shewmon 2004**, 175–188.

Fesmire S. 1995. Dramatic Rehearsal and the Moral Artist: A Deweyan Theory of Moral Understanding. *Transactions of the Charles S. Peirce Society,* **21**:568–97.

—— 2003. *John Dewey and Moral Imagination: Pragmatism in Ethics.* Indiana University Press.

Feudtner, Chris. 2007. Collaborative Communication in Pediatric Palliative Care: A Foundation for Problem-solving and Decision-making. *Pediatric Clinics of North America,* **54**:583–607.

Fins JJ. 2005. Rethinking Disorders of Consciousness: New Research and Its Implications. *Hastings Center Report,* **35**(2):22–4.

—— 2006. *A Palliative Ethic of Care: Clinical Wisdom at Life's End.* Jones and Bartlett.

—— et al. 1999. End-of-life Decision Making in the Hospital: Current Practice and Future Prospects. *Journal of Pain and Symptom Management,* **17**(1):6–15.

Foley K. 2002. Compassionate Care, Not Assisted Suicide. In **Foley** and **Hendin** 2002, 293–309.

—— and **Hendin H** (eds.). 2002. *The Case against Assisted Suicide: For the Right to End-of-Life Care.* Johns Hopkins University Press.

Frank A. 1991. *At the Will of the Body: Reflections on Illness.* Houghton Mifflin.

—— 1995. *The Wounded Storyteller: Body, Illness, and Ethics.* University of Chicago Press.

—— 1997. Enacting Illness Stories: When, What, and Why. **Nelson** 1997, 31–49.

Gale R. 1999. *The Divided Self of William James.* Cambridge University Press.

Galston WA. 2002. *Liberal Pluralism.* Cambridge University Press.

Ganzini, L, Goy ER, and **Dobscha, SK**. 2008. Prevalence of Depression and Anxiety in Patients Requesting Physicians' Aid in Dying: Cross Sectional Survey. *British Medical Journal,* **337**:973–5.

Gavin WJ. 1995. *Cuttin' the Body Loose.* Temple University Press.

———. 2003 [1999]. On " Tame" and "Untamed " Death: Jamesian Reflections. In **McGee 2003**, 93–108.

Gaylin W, Kass LR, Pellegrino ED, and **Siegler M**. 1988. Doctors Must Not Kill. *Journal of the American Medical Association,* **259**(14):2139–40.

Gert, Bernard. 2004. Common Morality: Deciding What to Do. Oxford University Press.

Giacino JT et al. 2002. The Minimally Conscious State: Definition and Diagnostic Criteria. *Neurology,* **58**:349–53.

Gill CJ. 1992. Suicide Intervention for People with Disabilities: A Lesson in Inequality. *Issues in Law & Medicine,* **8**:37–51.

Groves K. 2006. Justified Paternalism: The Nature of Beneficence in the Care of Demented Patients. *Penn Bioethics Journal,* **2**(2):17–20.

Grunau R. 2002. Early Pain in Preterm Infants. A Model of Long-Term Effects. *Clinical Perinatology,* **29**(3):373–94.

Hackler JC, Moseley R, and **Vawter DE** (eds.). 1989. *Advance Directives in Medicine.* Praeger.

Halevy, Amir. 2001. Beyond Brain Death? *Journal of Medicine and Philosophy,* **26**(5):493–502.

Halevy A and **Brody BA**. 1993. Brain Death: Reconciling Definitions, Criteria, and Tests. *Annals of Internal Medicine,* **119**:519–25.

Hamilton, NG. 2002. Oregon's Culture of Silence. In **Foley** and **Hendin** 2002, 175–91.

Hammes BJ, Klevan J, Kempf M, and **Williams MS**. 2005. Pediatric Advance Care Planning. *Journal of Palliative Medicine,* **8**(4):766–73.

Hardwig J. 1997a. Autobiography, Biography, and Narrative Ethics. In **Nelson 1997**, 50–64. Also in Hardwig 2000, 101–117.

———. 1997b. Is There a Duty to Die? *Hastings Center Report,* **27**(2):34–42. Also in **Hardwig** 2000, 119–136.

———. 2000. *Is There a Duty to Die? (and Other Essays in Medical Ethics).* Routledge.

Hester DM. 1998. Progressive Dying: Meaningful Act of Euthanasia and Assisted Suicide. *Journal of Medical Humanities,* **19**(4):279–98.

———. 2001. *Community As Healing: Pragmatist Ethics in Medical Encounters.* Rowman & Littlefield.

———. 2003 [1999]. Significance at the End of Life. In **McGee** 2003, 121–36.

———. 2007. Interests and Neonates: There Is More to the Story than We Explicitly Acknowledge. *Theoretical Medicine and Bioethics,* **28**(5): 357–72.

Himelstein BP, Hilden JM, Boldt AM, and **Weissman D**. 2004. *Pediatric Palliative Care. New England Journal of Medicine,* **350**(17):1752–60.

Hook S. 1974. *Pragmatism and the Tragic Sense of Life.* Basic Books.

Hook Sidney. 2002. The Ethics of Controversy. **Talisse R** and **Tempio R** (eds.), *The Essential Essays of Sidney Hook on Pragmatism, Democracy, and Freedom*. Prometheus Books, 289–95.

Hughes JJ. 2004. The Death of Death. In **Machado** and **Shewmon** 2004, 79–87.

Institutes of Medicine (IOM). 2002. *When Children Die: Improving Palliative and End-of-Life Care for Children and Their Families*. www.nap.edu/catalog/10390.html.

James W. 1977. *The Writings of William James: A Comprehensive Edition*. **McDermott JJ** (ed.). University of Chicago Press.

—— [1891]. The Moral Philosopher and the Moral Life. In **James** 1977, 610–29.

—— [1897]. "Radical Empiricism" from *The Will to Believe*. In **James** 1977, 134–6.

—— [1899a]. On a Certain Blindness in Human Beings. In **James** 1977, 629–45.

—— [1899b]. What Makes a Life Significant. In **James** 1977, 645–60.

—— [1904]. A World of Pure Experience. In **James** 1977, 194–214.

—— [1909]. "Radical Empiricism" from *The Meaning of Truth*. In **James** 1977, 136.

—— [1911]. Faith and the Right to Believe. In **James** 1977, 735–40.

—— 1902. *The Varieties of Religious Experience: A Study in Human Nature*. Longmans, Green.

Jennett B and **Plum F**. 1972. Persistent Vegetative State after Brain Damage. A Syndrome in Search of a Name. *Lancet*, **1**:734–7.

Jonas H. 1974. Against the Stream: Comments on Definition and Redefinition of Death. In *Philosophical Essays: From Ancient Creed to Technological Man*. **Jonas H** (ed.). Prentice Hall, 132–40.

Jotkowitz AB and **Glick S**. 2006. The Groningen Protocol: Another Perspective. *Journal of Medical Ethics*. **32**:157–8.

Kadish SH. 1992. Letting Patients Die: Legal and Moral Reflections. *California Law Review*, **80**(4):857–88.

Kamerman. 1988. *Death in the Midst of Life*. Prentice Hall.

Karakatsanis KG and **Tsanakas JN**. 2002. A Critique of the Concept of "Brain Death." *Issues in Law & Medicine*, **18**(2):127–42.

Kass LR. 2002. "I Will Give No Deadly Drug": Why Doctors Must Not Kill. In **Foley** and **Hendin** 2002, 17–40.

Kaufman SR. 2005. . . . *And a Time to Die: How American Hospitals Shape the End of Life*. Scribner.

Kerridge IH et al. 2002. Death, Dying and Donation: Organ Transplantation and the Diagnosis of Death. *Journal of Medical Ethics*, **28**:89–94.

King NMP. 1996. *Making Sense of Advance Directives*, revised ed. Georgetown University Press.

Kipnis K. 2004. When Are You Dead? *The Philosopher's Magazine*, Vol. 27.

Kleinman A. 1988. *The Illness Narratives*. Basic Books.

Kobylarz EJ and **Schiff ND**. 2004. Functional Imaging of Severely Brain-injured Patients: Process, Challenges, and Limitations. *Archives of Neurology*, **61**:1357–60.

Kon, AA. 2005. Discussing Nonsurgical Care with Parents: Newborns with Hypoplastic Left Heart Syndrome. *Newborn and Infant Nursing Review*, **5**(2):60–8.

——— 2007. Neonatal Euthanasia Is Unsupportable: The Groningen Protocol Should Be Abandoned. *Theoretical Medicine and Bioethics*, **28**(5):453–63.

———, **Ackerson L**, and **Lo B**. 2004. How Pediatricians Counsel Parents When no "Best-Choice" Management Exists: Lessons to be Learned from Hypoplastic Left Heart Syndrome. *Archives of Pediatric and Adolescent Medicine*. **158**(5):436–41.

Kopelman AE. 2006. Understanding, Avoiding, and Resolving End-of-Life Conflicts in the NICU. *Mount Sinai Journal of Medicine*, **73**(3):580–5.

Kopelman L. 1997. The Best-Interests Standard as Threshold, Ideal, and Standard of Reasonableness. *Journal of Medicine and Philosophy*, **22**:271–89.

——— 2005. Rejecting the Baby Doe Rules and Defending a "Negative" Analysis of the Best Interests Standard. *Journal of Medicine and Philosophy*, **30**:331–52.

Korein J and **Machado C**. 2004. Brain Death: Updating a Valid Concept for 2004. In **Machado** and **Shewmon** 2004, 1–14.

Kubler-Ross E. 1969. *On Death and Dying*. Macmillan.

Kuczewski MG. 1999. Commentary: Narrative Views of Personal Identity and Substituted Judgment in Surrogate Decision Making. *Journal of Law, Medicine & Ethics*, **27**:32–6.

Lachs J. 1994. When Abstract Moralizing Runs Amok. *Journal of Clinical Ethics*. **5**(1):10–3.

Lammi MH et al. 2005. The Minimally Conscious State and Recovery Potential: A Follow-Up Study 2 to 5 Years after Traumatic Brain Injury. *Archives of Physical Medicine and Rehabilitation*, **86**(4):746–54.

Lang CJG and **Heckman JG**. 2004. How Should Testing for Apnea Be Performed in Diagnosing Brain Death? In **Machado** and **Shewmon** 2004, 169–174.

Lantos JD. 2001. *The Lazarus Case*. Johns Hopkins University Press.

Laureys S, **Owen AM**, and **Schiff ND**. 2004. Brain Function in Coma, Vegetative State, and Related Disorders. *Lancet Neurology*, **3**(69):537–46.

Lee SJ et al. 2005. Fetal Pain: A Systematic Multidisciplinary Review of the Evidence. *Journal of the American Medical Association*, **294**(8):947–54.

Lewis P. 2000. The Logic of Christian Theology and the "Right" to Die. *Issues in Integrative Studies*, **18**:65–79.

Lizza JP. 2004. The Conceptual Basis for Brain Death Revisited: Loss of Organic Integration or Loss of Consciousness. In **Machado** and **Shewmon** 2004.

——— 2005. Potentiality, Irreversibility, and Death. *Journal of Medicine and Philosophy*, **30**:45–64.

Loewy EH and **Loewy RS**. 2000. *The Ethics of Terminal Care: Orchestrating the End of Life.* Kluwer Academic.

Machado C and **Shewmon DA** (eds.). 2004. *Brain Death and Disorders of Consciousness* (Advances in Experimental Medicine and Biology, vol. 550).

Mahowald MB. 2003. On Helping People Die: A Pragmatic Account. In **McGee** 2003, 109–120.

McAiley LG and **Daly BJ**. 2002. Baby Grace (case study with commentaries). *Hastings Center Report,* **32**(1):12–15.

McAiley LG, Hudson-Barr DC, Gunning RS, and **Rowbottom LA**. 2000. The Use of Advance Directives with Adolescents. *Pediatric Nursing,* **26**(5):471–80.

McDermott JJ. 1986. *Streams of Experience: Reflections on the History and Philosophy of American Culture.* University of Massachusetts Press.

——— 2006. Afterword: You Are Really Able. In *Experience As Philosophy: On the Work of John J. McDermott.* **Campbell J** and **Hart RE** (eds.). 2006. Fordham University Press, 237–271.

McGee GE (ed.). 2003. *Pragmatic Bioethics,* 2nd edition, MIT Press. First edition, Vanderbilt University Press, 1999.

Mead GH. 1938. *The Philosophy of the Act.* **Morris CW** (ed.). University of Chicago Press.

——— 1962 [1934]. *Mind, Self, and Society from the Standpoint of a Social Behaviorist.* **Morris CM** (ed.). University of Chicago Press.

Miller FG, Fins JJ, and **Snyder L**. 2002. Assisted Suicide and Refusal of Treatment: Valid Distinction or Distinction without a Difference? In **Snyder** and **Caplan** 2002, 17–28.

Miller RB. 2003. *Children, Ethics, and Modern Medicine.* Indiana University Press.

Misak C. 2000. *Truth, Politics, Morality: Pragmatism and Deliberation.* Routledge.

Montell, M and **Lantos J**. 2002. The Karamazov Complex: Dostoevsky and DNR Orders. *Perspectives in Biology and Medicine,* **45**:190–9.

Multi-society Task Force Report on PVS. 1994. Medical Aspects of the Persistent Vegetative State. *New England Journal of Medicine,* **330**:1499–508, 1572–9.

Murphy DM and **Pritchard J**. 2005. Letter to the Editor (Euthanasia in Severely Impaired Newborns). *New England Journal of Medicine.* **352**(22):2353–4.

Myers GE. 1986. *William James: His Life and Thought.* Yale University Press.

Naccache L. 2006. Is She Conscious? *Science,* **313**:1395–6.

Nelson HL (ed.). 1997. *Stories and Their Limits: Narrative Approaches to Bioethics.* Routledge.

Nelson HL and **Nelson JL**. 1995. *The Patient in the Family.* Routledge.

Newton MJ. 1999. Precedent Autonomy: Life-Sustaining Intervention and the Demented Patient. *Cambridge Quarterly of Healthcare Ethics,* **8**(2):189–99.

Nuffield Council on Bioethics. 2006. *Critical Care Decisions in Fetal and Neonatal Medicine: Ethical Issues.* http://www.nuffieldbioethics.org/go/ourwork/neonatal/publication_406.html.

Nuland SB. 1993. *How We Die: Reflections on Life's Final Chapter.* Alfred A. Knopf.

Oliver P. 2001. *Springs of Delight: The Return to Life.* Vanderbilt University Press.

Orentlicher D and **Snyder L**. 2002. Can Assisted Suicide Be Regulated? In **Snyder** and **Caplan** 2002, 55–69.

Osiovich H, Phillipos E, Byrne P, and **Robertson M**. Hypoplastic Left Heart Syndrome: "To Treat or Not To Treat." *Journal of Perinatology,* **20**(6): 363–5.

Owen AM et al. 2006. Detecting Awareness in the Vegetative State. *Science,* **313**:1402.

Paris JJ, Graham N, Schreiber MD, and **Goodwin M**. 2006a. Approaches to End-of-Life Decision-Making in the NICU: Insights from Dostoevsky's The Grand Inquisitor. *Journal of Perinatology,* **26**:389–91.

_____ 2006b. Has the Emphasis on Autonomy Gone Too Far? Insights from Dostoevsky on Parental Decision-Making in the NICU. *Cambridge Quarterly of Healthcare Ethics.* **15**:147–51.

Paris JJ and **Moreland MP**. 1998. A Catholic Perspective on Physician-assisted Suicide. In **Battin, Rhodes**, and **Silvers** 1998, 324–33.

Pellegrino ED. 1979. Anatomy of a Clinical Judgment: Some Notes on Right Reason and Right Action. In *Clinical Judgment: A Critical Appraisal.* **Engelhardt HT** et al. (eds.). D. Reidel Publishing, 169–194.

Plato. 1997. *Plato: Complete Works.* **Cooper JM** (ed.). Hackett.

Potts M. 2001. A Requiem for Whole Brain Death: A Response to D. Alan Shewmon's "The Brain and Somatic Integration." *Journal of Medicine and Philosophy,* **26**(5):479–491.

_____ **Byrne PA** and **Nilges RG** (eds.). 2000. *Beyond Brain Death: The Case against Brain Based Criteria for Human Death.* Kluwer Academic.

Prado, CG. 2008. *Choosing to Die: Elective Death and Multiculturalism.* Cambridge University Press.

President's Commission for the Study of Ethical Problems in Medicine and Biomedical and Behavioral Research. 1981. *Defining Death.*

_____ 1983. *Deciding to Forego Life-Sustaining Treatment.*

President's Council on Bioethics. 2008. *Controversies in the Determination of Death: A White Paper by the President's Council on Bioethics.* http://www.bioethics.gov/reports/death/determination_of_death_report.pdf.

Puchalski M and **Hummel P**. 2002. The Reality of Neonatal Pain. *Advances in Neonatal Care,* **2**(5):233–44.

Quill TE and **Battin MP** (eds.). 2004. *Physician-Assisted Dying: The Case for Palliative Car and Patient Choice.* Johns Hopkins University Press.

Quill TE, Lee BC, and **Nunn SJ**. 2002. Palliative Treatments of Last Resort: Choosing the Least Harmful Alternative. In **Snyder** and **Caplan** 2002, 70–83.

Ramsay S. 1996. British Group Presents Vegetative-State Criteria, *The Lancet*, **347**(9009):917.

Randall F and **Downie RS**. 1999. *Palliative Care Ethics: A Companion for all Specialties*, 2nd ed. Oxford University Press.

Rappaport ZH and **Rappaport IT**. 2004. Brain Death and Organ Transplantation: Concepts and Principles in Judaism. In **Machado** and **Shewmon** 2004, 133–38.

Rawls J. 1996. *Political Liberalism*. Columbia University Press.

Rich BA. 1997. Prospective Autonomy and Critical Interests: A Narrative Defense of the Moral Authority of Advance Directives. *Cambridge Quarterly of Healthcare Ethics*, **6**(2):138–47.

Rieff D. 2008. *Swimming in the Sea of Death: A Son's Memoir*. Simon & Schuster.

Robertson J. 1975. Involuntary Euthanasia of Defective Newborns. *Stanford Law Review*. **27**:246–61.

Rosner F. 1999. The Definition of Death in Jewish Law. In **Younger** 1999, 210–22.

Ross LF. 1997. *Health Care Decision-Making By Children*. Hastings Center Report. **27**(6):41–45.

—— 1998. *Children, Families, and Health Care Decision Making*. Oxford University Press.

—— 2009. Against the Tide: Arguments against Respecting a Minor's Refusal of Efficacious Life-Saving Treatment. *Cambridge Quarterly of Healthcare Ethics*, **18**(3):302–15.

Ross LF and **Frader JE**. 2009. Hypoplastic Left Heart Syndrome: A Paradigm Case for Examining Conscientious Objection in Pediatric Practice. *Pediatrics*, **155**(1):12–15.

Roth JK. 1969. *Freedom and the Moral Life: The Ethics of William James*. Westminster Press.

Rubin SB. 1998. *When Doctors Say No: The Battleground of Medical Futility*. Indiana University Press.

Sacks O. 1990. *Awakenings*. Harper Perennial.

Schiff ND et al. 2002. Residual Cerebral Activity and Behavioural Fragments Can Remain in the Persistently Vegetative Brain. *Brain*, **125**:1210–34.

Schneiderman LJ and **Jecker NS**. 1995. *Wrong Medicine: Doctors, Patients, and Futile Treatment*. Johns Hopkins University Press.

Seifert J. 2004. Consciousness, Mind, Brain, and Death. In **Machado** and **Shewmon** 2004, 61–78.

Seigfried CH. 1990. *William James's Radical Reconstruction of Philosophy*. SUNY Press.

Selzer R. 1990. *Imagine a Woman & Other Tales*. Random House.

—— 1992. *Down from Troy*. Little, Brown.

Shade, Patrick. 2001. *Habits of Hope: A Pragmatic Theory*. Vanderbilt University Press.

Shavelson Lonny. 1995. *A Chosen Death: The Dying Confront Assisted Suicide*. Simon & Schuster.

Shewmon DA. 1998. "Brainstem Death," "Brain Death" and Death: A Critical Re-evaluation of the Purported Equivalence. *Issues in Law and Medicine,* **14**(2):125–145.

———— 2001. The Brain and Somatic Integration: Insights into the Standard Biological Rationale for Equating "Brain Death" with Death. *Journal of Medicine and Philosophy,* **26**(5):457–78.

———— 2004. The ABC of PVS: Problems of Definition. *In Machado and Shewmon* **2004**, 215–228.

———— and **Shewmon ES**. 2004. The Semiotics of Death and Its Medical Implications. In **Machado** and **Shewmon** 2004, 89–114.

Silvers A. 1998. Protecting the Innocents for Physician-Assisted Suicide. In **Battin, Rhodes,** and **Silvers** 1998, 133–48.

Smith WJ. 1997. *Forced Exit: Euthanasia, Assisted Suicide, and the New Duty to Die.* Encounter Books.

Snyder L and **Caplan A** (eds.). 2002. *Assisted Suicide: Finding Common Ground.* Indiana University Press.

———— and **Faber-Langedoen K**. 2002. The Role of Guidelines in the Practice of Physician-Assisted Suicide. In **Snyder** and **Caplan** 2002, 29–43.

Stoddard S. 1991. *The Hospice Movement: A Better Way of Caring for the Dying,* revised edition. Vintage Books.

Sulmasy Daniel. 1995. Managed Care, Managed Death. *Archives of Internal Medicine,* **155**(2):133–36.

SUPPORT Principal Investigators. 1995. A Controlled Trial to Improve Care for Seriously Ill Hospitalized Patients: The Study to Understand Prognoses and Preferences for Outcomes and Risks of Treatments (SUPPORT). *Journal of the American Medical Association,* **274**(20):1591–8.

Talisse RB. 2004. Can Value Pluralists Be Comprehensive Liberals? Galston's Liberal Pluralism. *Contemporary Political Theory,* **3**(2):127–39.

———— 2005. *Democracy after Liberalism: Pragmatism and Deliberative Politics.* Routledge.

———— and **Aikin SF**. 2008. *Pragmatism: A Guide for the Perplexed.* Continuum.

———— and **Hester DM**. 2004. *On James: Philosophy As Vision.* Wadsworth.

Teno JM et al. 2007. Association between Advance Directives and Quality of End-of-Life Care: A National Study. *Journal of the American Geriatrics Association,* **55**(2):189–94.

Torke AM et al. 2008. Substituted Judgment: The Limitations of Autonomy in Surrogate Decision Making. *Journal of General Internal Medicine,* **23**(9):1514–7.

Truog R. 1997. Is It Time to Abandon Brain Death? *Hastings Center Report,* **27**(1):29–37.

Valdiserri, R. 1994. *Gardening in Clay: Reflections on AIDS.* Cornell University Press.

van der Heide A et al. 2007. End-of-Life Practices in the Netherlands under the Euthanasia Act. *New England Journal of Medicine,* **356**:1957–65.

Veatch RM. 1976. *Death, Dying and the Biological Revolution: Our Last Quest for Responsibility.* Yale University Press.

_____ 1999. The Conscience Clause: How Much Individual Choice in Defining Death Can Our Society Tolerate? In **Younger** 1999, 137–60.

_____ 2005. The Death of Whole-Brain Death: The Plague of the Disaggregators, Somaticists, and Mentalists. *Journal of Medicine and Philosophy.* **30**:353–78.

Verhagen AAE and **Sauer PJJ**. 2005a. The Groningen Protocol – Euthanasia in Severely Ill Newborns. *New England Journal of Medicine*, **352**(10):959–62.

_____ 2005b. End-of-Life Decisions in Newborns: An Approach from the Netherlands. *Pediatrics*, **1116**(3):736–9.

Verhey A. 1998. A Protestant Perspective on Ending Life. In **Battin, Rhodes**, and **Silvers** 1998, 347–61.

Walker MU. 1998. *Moral Understandings: A Feminist Study of Ethics*. Routledge.

Weir RF (ed.). 1997. *Physician-Assisted Suicide*. Indiana University Press.

Wharton RH, Levine KR, Buka S, Emanuel L. 1996. Advance care planning for children with special health care needs: a survey of parental attitudes. *Pediatrics*, **97**(5):682–7.

Wijdicks EFM. 2001. The Diagnosis of Brain Death. *New England Journal of Medicine*, **344**(16):1215–21.

_____ 2006. Minimally Conscious State vs. Persistent Vegetative State: The Case of Terry (Wallis) vs. the Case of Terri (Schiavo). *Mayo Clinic Proceedings*, **81**(9):1155–8.

_____ and **Cranford RE**. 2005. Clinical Diagnosis of Prolonged States of Impaired Consciousness in Adults. *Mayo Clinic Proceedings*, **80**(8):1037–46.

Wild J. 1980. *The Radical Empiricism of William James*. Greenwood.

Wilson KG et al. 2007. Desire for Euthanasia or Physician-Assisted Suicide in Palliative Cancer Care. *Health Psychology*, **26**(3):314–23.

_____ 2000. Attitudes of Terminally Ill Patients Toward Euthanasia and Physician-Assisted Suicide. *Archives of Internal Medicine*, **160**(16):2454–60.

Woodbridge FJE. 1929. *Son of Apollo: Themes of Plato*. Houghton Mifflin.

Young, Robert. 2008. *Medically Assisted Death*. Cambridge University Press.

Younger SJ, Arnold RM. 2001. Philosophical Debates about the Definition of Death: Who Cares? *Journal of Medicine and Philosophy*, **26**(5):527–37.

_____ and **Schapiro R** (eds.). 1999. *The Definition of Death: Contemporary Controversies*. Johns Hopkins University Press.

Zaner RM. 1988. *Ethics and the Clinical Encounter*. Prentice Hall.

Zeman A. 1997. Persistent Vegetative State. *Lancet*, **350**:795–9.

Zucker MB and **Zucker HD** (eds.). 1997. *Medical Futility and the Evaluation of Life-Sustaining Interventions*. Cambridge University Press.

Index